Shoot
ANNUAL 2000

IPC MAGAZINES
24th FLOOR
KING'S REACH TOWER
STAMFORD STREET
LONDON SE1 9LS
TEL: 0171-261-6287
FAX: 0171-261-6019

EDITOR
ANDY WINTER

ART EDITOR
CHRIS DAVIES

DEPUTY ART EDITOR
COLIN HALLIDAY

PICTURE EDITOR
DUNCAN BOND

CONTRIBUTORS
JULIAN PRYKE
JUDITH ADDELSON
KRISTAN REED
DUKE METTLE

EDITOR'S SECRETARY
JUNE HISCOCK

PHOTOGRAPHS SUPLLIED BY
ALLSPORT, EMPICS & ACTION
IMAGES

PRODUCTION MANAGER
TOM JENNINGS

ASSOCIATE BOOK PUBLISHER
RACHEL PEARCE

PUBLISHER
SEAN SINGLETON

MANAGING DIRECTOR
ANDY McDUFF

SHOOT SUBSCRIPTIONS HOTLINE
01622-778-778
(9am-7pm – seven days a week)

BACK ISSUES DEPARTMENT
0181-503-0588

LICENCING ENQUIRIES
+44 (0)171-261-7715

©**IPC Magazines 1999**

ipc
music●sport

Distributed by Pedigree Books Limited,
The Old Rectory, Matford Lane, Exeter,
Devon EX2 4PS.

CARLING
CHAMPIONS 1998-99

CHAMPIONS

Man United, Rangers, Totten
– 1999's greatest clubs and th

ONS 1999

n, Lazio, Parma

rophies they won!

UNITED WIN

You'd think a team that had already done a league and cup double twice wouldn't be that hungry for honours. Nothing could have been further from the truth for Man United, who, after winning nothing in 1998, were determined to refill their trophy cabinet with as much silverware as they could!

THRILLING TITLE CHASE

After a thrilling Premiership battle with Arsenal and Chelsea, Alex Ferguson's side claimed the Premiership – their fifth title win in seven years. Although the likes of Roy Keane, David Beckham and Peter Schmeichel had been as brilliant as ever for The Red Devils, it was Ferguson's expensive new signings – Dutch defender Jaap Stam (£10 million) and striker Dwight Yorke (£12.6 million) – who received the most attention. Both were in terrific form all season, with Yorke hitting 18 of Man United's 80 Premiership goals. The race for the title went down to the last day of the season but Arsenal's 1-0 win over Aston Villa proved worthless as United cruised to a 2-1 win over Tottenham. It was the first time United had clinched the Championship at Old Trafford which, according to Ferguson, made victory sweeter than ever!

Champions... again!

Dwight Yorke and Andy Cole proved to be a lethal strike partnership last season.

It's five titles in seven years for United!

It took him a while but Ted finally got his hands on some silverware!

Many fans and pundits thought Becks should have been Player Of The Year.

THE LOT!

Keane, Schmeichel and May celebrate another double.

Manager Alex Ferguson holds aloft the FA Cup.

Newcastle's second FA Cup Final defeat in a row is more than some of their players can bear.

Sheringham came off the subs' bench to fire United into the lead.

David Beckham helps Teddy Sheringham celebrate his goal against Newcastle.

Welsh wing wizard Ryan Giggs whoops it up at Wembley.

United's goalscorers, Sheringham and Scholes.

TOON TROUNCED AT WEMBLEY

Next up was the FA Cup Final against Newcastle. Ruud Gullit's men were keen to put the previous year's final, where they had been outclassed and easily defeated by Arsenal, behind them, but froze on the big occasion once again. Goals from substitute Teddy Sheringham and England star Paul Scholes polished off the Geordies making United the first team in history to claim three domestic doubles.

INJURY TIME HEAVEN

But United weren't finished there and went to face German giants Bayern Munich in Barcelona confident they could lift their first European Cup for 31 years. The Red Devils got off to the worst possible start after the Germans took the lead in the sixth minute thanks to a Mario Bassler free-kick. But even without the suspended Paul Scholes and Roy Keane, United were not to be denied yet another taste of glory. Deep into injury time substitute Teddy Sheringham fired a Manchester equaliser and barely 60 seconds later another sub, Ole Gunnar Solskjaer, broke Bayern hearts with an incredible winner. Fergie's boys had done it — three trophies, including the European Cup, in one season. The big question now, is what on earth are they going to do for an encore?!

Sub Ole Solskjaer seems to be quite happy about something.

Ole Solskjaer seals United's amazing injury time comeback with the winner.

Ryan Giggs helped inspire United's fight back against the Germans.

Schmeichel: United's best ever 'keeper?

Peter Schmeichel's last ever game for United proved quite eventful!

The Neville Brothers proudly show off United's European Cup.

Dutch defender Jaap Stam was in commanding form in the Champions League Final.

THE TREBLE: HOW UNITED DID IT

Teddy scored United's opening goal against Newcastle in the Cup Final and repeated the trick in Barcelona.

PREMIERSHIP

	P	W	D	L	F	A	Pts
1. Man United	38	22	13	3	80	37	79
2. Arsenal	38	22	12	4	59	17	78
3. Chelsea	38	20	15	3	57	30	75

FA CUP FINAL

MAN UNITED (1) 2 Sheringham (11), Scholes (53)
NEWCASTLE (0) 0

EUROPEAN CUP FINAL

MAN UNITED (0) 2 Sheringham (90), Solskjaer (90)
BAYERN MUNICH (1) 1 Bassler (6)

UNITED'S STAR OF THE SEASON

Becks finished a truly brilliant season with a fine performance against Bayern.

DAVID BECKHAM

After his sending off against Argentina in 1998's World Cup Finals the knives were out for Becks. Some even suggested his United career was over and that he should go and play abroad. Beckham had other ideas however and ended up playing the best football of his career last season. He may only have scored six league goals himself but his free-kicks, crosses and inch perfect passes helped United hit the back of the net 80 times last season. He was also The Red Devils' best player in the European Cup Final against Bayern Munich. His never-say-die attitude and tireless running helped United come from behind in that game to record an incredible win.

UNITED'S TROPHIES UNDER FERGIE

EUROPEAN CUP: 1999 (1)	
LEAGUE TITLE: 1993, 1994, 1996, 1997, 1999 (5)	
FA CUP: 1990, 1994, 1996, 1999 (4)	
EUROPEAN CUP WINNERS' CUP: 1991 (1)	
LEAGUE CUP: 1992 (1)	
TOTAL: 12	

RANGERS' SCO

Rangers had a terrible time in 1998. Not only did the end of the season witness the departures of long serving boss Walter Smith and scoring legend Ally McCoist but the club had finished the season with nothing. Arch rivals Celtic had taken the League Cup and more importantly the Scottish League title, denying Gers an unprecedented ten championships in a row. 1999 has been a very different story however. Under new manager Dick Advocaat the boys in blue won the lot – the title, the Scottish Cup and the League Cup, while it was The Bhoys' turn to stare at an empty trophy cabinet.

GERS SQUEAK PAST SAINTS

St Johnstone had conceded 11 goals in their last two matches against Gers so the outcome of the League Cup Final was never really in doubt. However, Rangers struggled to really take command of the game and only squeaked past their Scottish Premier League rivals 2-1, thanks to first half goals from Stephane Guivarc'h and Jorge Albertz. But the nature of the win didn't matter to the players or the fans – the first piece of silverware of the season had been won!

Striker Rod Wallace on the attack against St Johnstone.

Jorge Albertz grabs Rangers' League Cup Final winner.

THE SCOTTISH FOOTBALL LEAGUE CUP WINNER

Another team in red won three trophies last season, who were they again?

Lorenzo Amoruso lifts Rangers' first piece of silverware of the season aloft.

Arthur Numan (Rangers) tackles St Johnstone's Phillip Scott.

Gers celebrate their League Cup Final win.

Shoot

TTISH TREBLE

Dick Advocaat and his boys make it ten titles in 11 years!

Champions of Scotland.

Dick Advocaat and the Scottish Championship trophy.

Neil McCann puts Rangers ahead in the Old Firm derby against Celtic.

BANK OF SCOTLAND

Scott Marshall and Neil McCann enjoy a bit of wrestling!

The sweet smell of success – Rangers in a party mood!

WAR AT PARKHEAD

To keep their slim title hopes alive Celtic had to beat Rangers in the two's final league encounter of the season. In their 111 year rivalry, Gers had never managed to win the title at Parkhead – until now. Rangers' 3-0 victory over The Bhoys was full of incident including three sendings off and, most notably, an injury to referee Hugh Dallas when a coin, thrown by a Celtic fan, hit him on the head leaving a wound which required stitches. Gers' three goals from Neil McCann (2) and a Jorge Albertz penalty wrapped up the win and the title.

IN HEAVEN AT HAMPDEN

Rangers completed their clean sweep of trophies with another victory over Celtic, this time in the Scottish Cup Final at the new Hampden Park. Former Leeds striker Rod Wallace scored the decisive goal early in the second half, his 27th in all competitions for the season. The game was refereed by Hugh Dallas, the man in black who'd been hit with a coin in the two sides' last meeting. Thankfully the game passed off without serious incident this time and Rangers' revenge over their old rivals was complete. They were once again Kinds Of Scotland!

Are you watching Celtic? Rangers and the Scottish Cup.

Former Blackburn star Colin Hendry with the Scottish Cup.

Rockin' Rod with the trophy that completed Gers' treble.

Dick Advocaat, Giovanni van Bronckhorst and assistant manager Bert van Lingen at Hampden.

Celtic's Regi Blinker battles Derek McInnes of Rangers for possession.

Mahe and Stubbs (Celtic) go up for a high ball with Hendry and Amoruso (Rangers).

Rod Wallace breaks Celtic hearts with his Cup winner.

THE TREBLE: HOW RANGERS DID IT

Arthur Numan might look daft but at least he's happy!

SCOTTISH PREMIER LEAGUE

	P	W	D	L	GF	GA	Pts
1. Rangers	36	23	8	5	78	31	77
2. Celtic	36	21	8	7	84	35	71
3. St Johnstone	36	15	12	9	39	38	57

SCOTTISH CUP FINAL

RANGERS (0) 1 Wallace (49)
CELTIC (0) 0

SCOTTISH LEAGUE CUP

RANGERS (2) 2 Guivarc'h (6), Albertz (37)
ST JOHNSTONE (1) 1 Dasovic (8)

RANGERS' STAR OF THE SEASON

Rangers' striker Rod Wallace – three trophies and 27 goals.

ROD WALLACE

When new Gers manager Dick Advocaat signed Wallace on a free transfer from Leeds in the summer of 1998 no one could have predicted the impact he'd make on Scottish football. The 30-year-old striker had found himself increasingly out of the picture at Elland Road and had suffered a few poor seasons in front of goal. Once he moved to Ibrox, however, Wallace soon established himself as one of Scotland's finest hitmen, finishing second only to Celtic's world class forward Henrik Larsson in the end of season goalscoring stakes. Wallace had been lethal all season bagging 26 goals. He completed a memorable nine months for both himself and his team by netting number 27, the winner against Celtic in the Scottish Cup Final. He clinched the treble in the process.

RANGERS

EIGHT YEARS AFTER THEIR LAST TROPHY SPURS FINALLY MADE IT TO WEMBLEY AGAIN UNDER NEW BOSS GEORGE GRAHAM.

TOTTENHAM BACK O

When ex-Arsenal boss George Graham took over at Tottenham many fans weren't happy. They soon cheered up when he led them to Worthington Cup glory though! Tottenham hadn't had as much of a sniff of a trophy since their FA Cup triumph back in 1991 so a cup or two in the White Hart Lane cabinet was well overdue.

Graham joined Tottenham from Leeds as boss back in October 1998 after the sacking of Christian Gross. But not even Spurs' most committed fans could have believed how quickly he turned things round.

The Final itself was poor and even double Player Of The Year winner David Ginola couldn't bring it to life. In fact, before Tottenham's winner two minutes into injury time the only talking point had come when Spurs' Justin Edinburgh had been sent off.

But as extra-time approached Les Ferdinand fed the ball out to Stefen Iversen who took it past defender Steve Walsh before firing on goal. Leicester 'keeper Kasey Keller parried his shot but Allan Neilsen reacted first to push the ball into the net and clinch victory for George Graham's men.

Tottenham's Stephen Freund holds off Neil Lennon of Leicester.

Allan Neilsen heads Spurs' last gasp winner.

The Spurs lads celebrate their first trophy for eight years.

WINNERS 1999

WINNERS 1999

Matt Elliott scraps with Les Ferdinand for possession.

Worthington cup 1999

Defender Sol Campbell takes a swig out of the Worthington Cup.

Handbags at ten paces between Justin Edinburgh and Robbie Savage!

THE GLORY TRAIL!

Tottenham's Justin Edinburgh gets his marching orders.

George Graham celebrates his first trophy with Spurs.

Double Player Of The Year, David Ginola, salutes the fans.

Man Of The Match Allan Neilsen with his award alongside George Graham and the Worthington Cup.

Yessss! Spurs are finally back in the big time.

HOW TOTTENHAM GOT TO THE FINAL

ROUND TWO (1ST LEG)
BRENTFORD   3-2

ROUND TWO (2ND LEG)
BRENTFORD   3-2

ROUND THREE
NORTHAMPTON   3-1

ROUND FOUR
LIVERPOOL   3-1

ROUND FIVE
MAN UNITED   3-1

SEMI-FINAL (1ST LEG)
WIMBLEDON   0-0

SEMI-FINAL (2ND LEG)
WIMBLEDON   1-0

MAN UNITED MIGHT HAVE WON THE EUROPEAN CUP BUT ITALIAN SIDES, PARMA AND LAZIO, EMERGED VICTORIOUS IN EUROPE'S TWO OTHER MAJOR CUP COMPS!

ITALIAN TEAMS DOMIN

When a British team wins a European trophy its always a big deal, but to Italian sides it has become second nature. Leading up to this year's European finals Italian clubs had won 14 European trophies in the last ten years, including five European Cups and seven UEFA Cups. It was little surprise then when Parma and Lazio both made it to Euro finals this year.

PERFECT PARMA

Parma may have had a disappointing time of it in the Italian league last season but more than made up for it by winning their second UEFA Cup in just five seasons. They simply proved too strong for French outfit Marseille, who were hit by injuries to key players. Parma were 2-0 up by half-time with goals from Hernan Crespo and Paolo Vanoli. They wrapped the game up early in the second half when Argentinian Juan Veron and World Cup winner Lilian Thuram combined to put Enrico Chiesa through on goal.

Marseille's Frederic Brando gets stuck into Juan Veron of Parma.

Parma are well chuffed after their 3-0 thumping of Marseille.

Goalscorer Enrico Chiesa chased by Marseille's Pierre Issa.

Parma players battle it out to get their hands on the UEFA Cup.

Parma's mighty yellow after the final whistle

"This is coming home with me!" Parma skipper Roberto Sensini makes off with the cup.

TE IN EUROPE... AGAIN!

Chilean Marcelo Salas plants a kiss on Lazio's Cup...

...as does Pavel Nedved!

The Lazio boys celebrate their win by sitting on the floor!

Lazio clinch victory with an 81st minute winner.

Pavel Nedved, the scorer of Lazio's winner, celebrates.

EUROPEAN CUP WINNERS' CUP FINAL	
LAZIO (1) 2	Vieri (7), Nedved (81)
R. MALLORCA (1) 1	Dani (11)

UEFA CUP FINAL	
PARMA (2) 3	Crespo (25), Vanoli (36), Chiesa (55)
MARSEILLE (0) 0	

LAZIO TRIUMPHANT

The last ever Cup Winners' Cup final was between Lazio and Spanish outfit Real Mallorca, who had dumped holders Chelsea out of the competition at the semi-final stage. And once again it was the Italians that triumphed. The Rome side got off to the best possible start when Man Of The Match Christian Vieri fired them ahead after just seven minutes. However, Mallorca refused to give up so quickly and four minutes later equalised through Dani. The game looked set to go into extra-time, but with just nine minutes on the clock Vieri flicked a header onto Nedved who clinched the win with a fine shot. Lazio had been beaten 3-0 in the UEFA Cup final by Inter Milan the season before so this piece of European glory was well overdue!

the greatest elland road stars from the past and present. Plus one to watch for the future!

PAST
ERIC CANTONA

The temperamental star's brief 12-month stay at Leeds was enough to help the success starved club to the 1991/92 League title – their first for 18 years. Perhaps the most influential and gifted foreign player to grace the English game, Cantona had originally arrived in England from Nimes for a trial with Sheff Wed. However, when that deal fell through the Yorkshire side snapped him up. Sadly for Leeds fans he eventually joined Man United after a clash with manager Howard Wilkinson.

JONATHAN WOODGATE

Another fine Elland Road youth product. Joined the club at 13, won the FA Youth Cup at 16 and has captained the England under-18 side. Repaid boss O'Leary's faith last season with a series of confident and assured perfomances at the heart of the Leeds defence. Equally at home at right back, Woodgate made his full England debut last summer v Bulgaria.

PRESENT

JIMMY FLOYD HASSELBAINK

Jimmy was bought by then Leeds manager George Graham from Portuguese outfit Boavista in 1997 after hitting 20 goals in 29 league appearances in one season. The Dutch international striker hasn't been quite as prolific in the Premiership but his goal haul during the two full seasons he's been at Elland Road is still impressive – 40 in 89 appearances in all competitions. It's certainly been enough to propel the Yorkshire side into Europe and make them one of the top-flight's most exciting, successful teams.

FUTURE

A TO Z

NEWCASTLE UNITED

A IS FOR APPEARANCES
Scottish 'keeper Jim Lawrence holds The Magpies appearance record – 496 between 1904 and 1922.

B IS FOR Peter Beardsley
One of the modern-day Newcastle greats. Beardsley arrived at Newcastle in 1983 and ended up helping them into the top division. He quit the club for Liverpool in 1987, but returned to the north-east in 1993 from Everton.

C IS FOR CUP FINALS
Newcastle have appeared in no less than 13 FA Cup finals. Sadly, they've gone home disappointed seven times and haven't won at Wembley since 1955.

D IS FOR DARLING OF THE TERRACES
Which is how the media referred to Brazilian hero Mirandinha, who arrived from Fluminese in 1987. Although he scored 23 goals in 55 games, he struggled to adapt to the English game and quit St James' Park in 1990.

E IS FOR ENGLAND BOSS KEVIN KEEGAN
King Kev still enjoys god-like status on Tyneside after his stint as boss, during which the club came back from the doldrums of Division Two in 1992 to become Premiership runners-up in '96.

F IS FOR FAIRS CUP
The old name for the UEFA Cup and the last major piece of silverware the club won – back in 1969.

G IS FOR GALLOWGATE
Which is how locals often refer to St James' Park. In the days before all-seater stadia, there was a huge open terrace behind one of the goals which was known as the Gallowgate End.

H IS FOR HISTORY
Newcastle were founded in 1881, originally known as Stanley, changing the name to Newcastle East End a year later. They became Newcastle United in 1892.

I IS FOR ITALY
The country where manager Ruud Gullit enjoyed most of his success with AC Milan as a player. He arrived at Chelsea to play under Glenn Hoddle in 1995 and took over as player/manager in 1996, steering them to the FA Cup in 1997. Sacked in 1998, Gullit took on the Newcastle job when Kenny Dalglish left in August 1998.

J IS FOR ST JAMES' PARK
The club's home since 1892. The biggest crowd at the ground, 68,386, watched the league game v Chelsea in Sept. 1930. The current capacity is 36,836, but there are plans to increase that to 50,000.

K IS FOR KING KENNY
Former Liverpool hero Kenny Dalglish took over as manager from Keegan in 1997 and despite steering the club to second in the league and to their first FA Cup Final in 24 years, he never hit it off with the fans. Few were upset when he left St James' in September 1998.

L IS FOR LOPING WINGER
Chris Waddle was plucked from non-league football and a job in a sausage factory to play on the wing in the famous '80s Newcastle side that included Kevin Keegan, Peter Beardsley and Terry McDermott. After breaking through into the England side, he was bought by Spurs in 1985 and played in the 1986 and 1990 World Cups.

C

D

E

M IS FOR MOST GOALS
In 1993/94 Andy Cole scored an amazing 41 times in all competitions. Cole was brought to the club from Bristol City and was a huge success in the north-east before he was sold to Man United in 1994.

N IS FOR Jimmy NAIL
The actor is among many celebrity Newcastle fans who also include Ant and Dec, Robson Green and the Prime Minister, Tony Blair.

O IS FOR OFF THE MARK
The fastest goal ever scored by a Newcastle player came after five seconds of a pre-season friendly against St Johnstone in 1975. The scorer was Malcolm MacDonald.

P IS FOR PROLIFIC PARTNERSHIP
The club's most successful striker pairing was Malcolm MacDonald and John Tudor. 'Super Mac' scored 121 goals in 228 appearances between 1969 and 1976, and Tudor bagged 58 goals in 184 games between 1971 and 1976.

Q IS FOR Mickey QUINN
Newcastle striker between 1989 and 1993. Despite his stocky build, Mickey was renowned for his ability to score goals from unbelievable positions. He notched 65 goals in 146 appearances for the club.

R IS FOR RECORD BUY
When Kevin Keegan signed Alan Shearer from Blackburn in the summer of 1996, he set a new British transfer record of 15 million.

S IS FOR STOPPERS
At West Ham in April 1986 three players donned the Toon goalkeeper's shirt during the course of the game. Regular 'keeper Martin Thomas was carried off injured, as was his replacement, Chris Hedworth, leaving Peter Beardsley in goal. The Hammers won 8-1.

T IS FOR TOP GOALSCORER
Jackie Milburn, the legendary Newcastle striker, has scored more goals for the club than anyone else, netting 177 times between 1946-57.

U IS FOR UNDERRATED
One of the best defenders to play for Newcastle was Frank Clark, who went on to manage Nott'm Forest and Man City. Between 1962 and 1975, he played 456 games as a full-back, only ever scoring one goal. Despite his reliability, he never received an international call-up.

V IS FOR Barry VENISON
Played for Newcastle in the early-mid '90s after joining from Liverpool. Most likely to be remembered for his vast array of dodgy jackets than for his footie skills.

W IS FOR big WIN
Newcastle recorded their biggest victory – 13-0 – on October 5, 1946 against Newport County.

X IS FOR X-RATED
Like the anti-Sunderland slogan on Sunderland star Lee Clark's t-shirt when he turned up at the 1999 FA Cup Final to cheer on his team's arch rivals, Toon. Suffice to say the Newcastle fan and former Magpies player was quickly transfer-listed when his actions came to light!

Y IS FOR YOUTH PLAYERS
Paul Gascoigne is surely the most gifted player to have come through the ranks at Newcastle. As a young player, Gazza had unbeliev-able dribbling ability and his quick thinking and intelligence made him the most wanted player in the land.

Z IS FOR ZEBRA STRIPES
Newcastle's famous black and white striped shirts were first introduced in 1894.

M

T

Y

FAMOUS WINS
ASTON VILLA

TEAMS
ASTON VILLA v MAN UNITED

MATCH
COCA-COLA CUP FINAL

VENUE
WEMBLEY

DATE
MARCH 27, 1994

STORY

The season of Man United's first FA Cup and League double could have so easily been a treble success story instead. Fergie's boys turned up at Wembley in April as red hot favourites to defeat Ron Atkinson's Villa side who had won just one of their previous six league games. However, such matters clearly didn't worry The Villains who went a goal up through striker Dalian Atkinson after 25 minutes. Dean Saunders made it 2-0 with 15 minutes left, and although Mark Hughes pulled one back for United their miserable afternoon was complete when Andrei Kanchelskis was sent off for hand ball and Dean Saunders scored with the resultant penalty to clinch the win. Victory was particularly sweet for Atkinson who'd been sacked by United in 1986.

FINAL SCORE
VILLA 3 UNITED 1

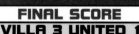

United's Andrei Kanchelskis sees red for deliberate handball.

After 25 minutes Dalian Atkinson slots home the opening goal of the game past a sprawling Les Sealey…

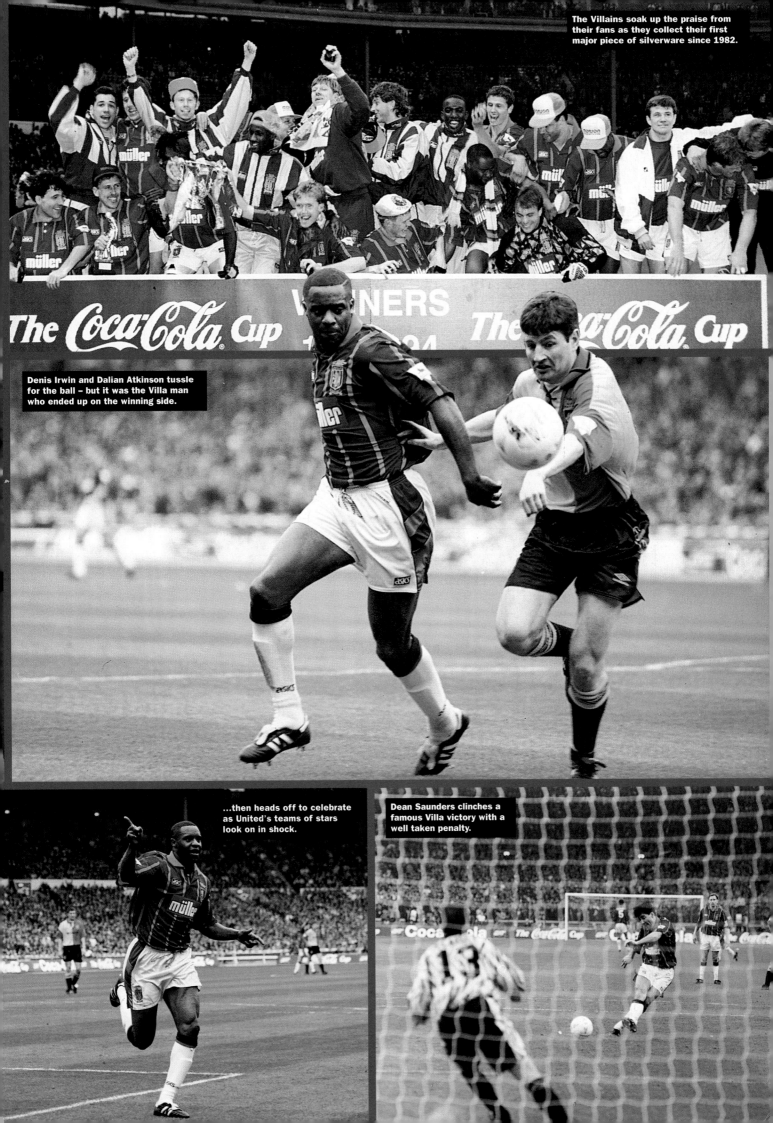

The Villains soak up the praise from their fans as they collect their first major piece of silverware since 1982.

Denis Irwin and Dalian Atkinson tussle for the ball – but it was the Villa man who ended up on the winning side.

...then heads off to celebrate as United's teams of stars look on in shock.

Dean Saunders clinches a famous Villa victory with a well taken penalty.

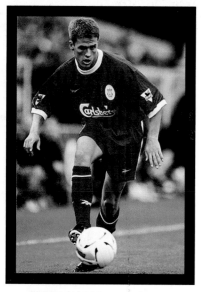

MICHAEL OWEN
LIVERPOOL

Michael Owen has rarely been out of the headlines since making his Liverpool debut against Wimbledon in 1997. The 20-year-old striker blasted his way into the England set up under Glenn Hoddle a year later and went on to make an enormous impact for England at the World Cup in France in 1998. His pace, skill and professional attitude make him one of the most exciting young stars in Europe.

THE STATS

- ⚽ SUPPORTS LIVERPOOL
- ⚽ BORN CHESTER 14/12/79
- ⚽ HEIGHT 5ft 8ins
- ⚽ WEIGHT 11st
- ⚽ TEAMS LIVERPOOL (1997-PRESENT)
- ⚽ INTERNATIONAL STATUS FULL ENGLAND INTERNATIONAL – DEBUT v CHILE, FEBRUARY 1998

1 — DONS DEBUT

Michael Owen makes his senior Liverpool debut against Wimbledon as a substitute on May 6, 1997. It's the penultimate game of the '96/97 season and Owen marks it with his first goal for the club. But it isn't enough as The Reds crash 2-1, finishing the season fourth.

OWEN MAKES HIS ENGLAND BOW

2 Owen makes his England debut in a pre-season World Cup friendly with Chile in early 1998 at Wembley. In doing so he becomes the youngest player to be capped by England this century at just 18 years and 59 days old. England lose the game to the South Americans 2-0.

TOP GUN

5 Liverpool thump champions Arsenal 4-0 in the last home game of the season and Owen clinches joint first place as the Premiership's top scorer. Blackburn's Chris Sutton and Coventry's Dion Dublin also hit 18 league goals for their clubs.

6 — GIVEN THE BOOT

...And the reward for being the Premiership's top scorer is the SHOOT/adidas Golden Boot. Here's Mike proudly showing his off, as he prepares to make some room in his trophy cupboard.

A FIRST GOAL FOR ENGLAND

7 Glenn Hoddle takes his men for a World Cup warm-up to Morocco where Mike gets on the scoresheet for his country for the first time. Hod's boys beat the Moroccans 1-0 and Owen clinches his place in the France '98 squad.

Shoot

③

YOUNG PLAYER OF 1998

There's little surprise when Michael is named by the Professional Footballers' Association as their Young Player Of The Year. He becomes the third Liverpool star to win the trophy following in the footsteps of Anfield scoring legend Ian Rush and Robbie Fowler (who has won it twice).

④

MIKE'S MARCHING ORDERS

Mike goes from hero to villain in the match at Old Trafford between Liverpool and Man United in 1998. The England youngster first grabs a 36th minute equaliser for The Reds but then gets himself red carded in the second-half following a crunching tackle on Ronny Johnsen. The game ends 1-1.

⑧

STAKING HIS CLAIM

Despite the clammer from England fans and the newspapers for him to play, manager Glenn Hoddle decides to keep Owen on the bench as the World Cup kicks off in France. He makes his first appearance in the tournament against Tunisia, on for Man United's Teddy Sheringham, as England cruise to a comfortable 2-0 win in their opening game.

⑩

THE GOAL THAT SHOOK THE WORLD

Mike's legendary solo World Cup goal came in the 16th minute of England's game v Argentina. With the score at 1-1, Owen picked the ball up near the half-way line and set off on one of his blistering runs. It took him past the static Argentine defence and ended with him chipping 'keeper Carlos Roa. Fantastic!

SAVIOUR – ALMOST!

Again on as a substitute Michael smashes home an 83rd minute equaliser against Romania. Sadly, his brilliant effort is all for nothing as a defensive blunder lets Chelsea star Dan Petrescu in at the other end to give the Romanians a 90th minute winner.

⑨

MICHAEL OWEN

YOU'LL NEVER WALK ALONE
LIVERPOOL FOOTBALL CLUB
EST 1892

LIVERPOOL

BACK TO BUSINESS

11

After the disappointment of England's World Cup exit it's back to business. Unlike many other top stars Mike gets straight back into the groove of Premiership life as he hits a hat-trick against Newcastle at St James' Park. For a time Liverpool look to be serious title contenders.

PERFECT PERSONALITY

12

Mike's amazing goalscoring feats with Liverpool and England see him catapulted into the big time. Lazio for the striker while he becomes the star every footie mad youngster wants to be. His brilliant 1998 is completed when he is named BBC Sports Personality Of The Year.

OLD TRAFFORD REVISITED

13

Although Michael didn't get himself sent off this time, he still left Old Trafford after Liverpool's FA Cup Fourth Round tie against Man United feeling very under the weather. Despite giving the Merseysiders an early lead, Owen is powerless as United strike back with two last gasp goals.

ENGLAND'S KOOL NEW KIT

14

Seeing Mike modelling the latest England kit with such confidence it's hard to imagine that he'd only made his national team debut a little over a year previously. In that incredibly brief time he's become England's most feared striker!

MICHAEL OWEN

LIVERPOOL

PAST
GARY LINEKER

Crisp-nabbing TV presenter Gary was a prolific top-flight striker in the early '80s, hitting 95 league goals for the midlands side in 194 appearances. He was also Filbert Street's top scorer four seasons in a row. He made his England debut while a regular in the Leicester side in 1984 as a sub against Scotland and went on to fall just one short of breaking Sir Bobby Charlton's all-time scoring record for his country. He moved to league champions Everton for £800,000 in 1985.

PRESENT
NEIL LENNON

Flame haired Lennon has carved out a reputation at Filbert Street as one of the most effective midfielders in the Premiership, covering every blade of grass for the full 90 minutes. Has also made his mark at International level with Northern Ireland. Boss and fellow countryman Martin O'Neill will find it tough to fend off the approaches for his midfield general as the season progresses.

Filbert Street's greatest hero from the past and another from the present. Plus a top youngster to watch in the future.

PAST PRESENT LEICES

FUTURE
EMILE HESKEY

Impressed just about everyone last season, including England boss Kevin Keegan who gave him his first full cap against Bulgaria. Boss O'Neill loves him: "He has performed miracles for us," he says. "Some of the turns he's made for the goals he's created have been exceptional." The only question hanging over Heskey's head is for how much longer The Foxes will be able to fend off big money offers for him.

FUTURE
TER CITY

A TO Z

A IS FOR record APPEARANCES
It's an honour which goes to ex-skipper, Billy Bonds, who played a total of 793 games for The Hammers between 1967 and 1988.

B IS FOR BOGOTA
The place in Colombia where West Ham legend Bobby Moore was arrested on a jewellery theft charge just before the World Cup of 1970. When it became clear that the allegations were part of a scam, he was soon released and allowed to rejoin the England squad.

C IS FOR international CAPS
Bobby Moore still holds the record number of caps for England, 108, the bulk of which he won as a West Ham player.

D IS FOR JULIAN DICKS
By far the most popular Hammers player in recent years. The tough-tacking left back was a regular for the best part of a decade, save one unhappy year at Liverpool, but his career is now almost over due to a bad knee injury.

E IS FOR EXTRAORDINARY
West Ham can boast 11 players who have scored 100 goals or more for the club. Top marksman is Vic Watson who played in the late 1920s and 1930s and scored 326 goals. The most recent addition to the list was Tony Cottee who netted 146 goals between 1983 and 1988.

F IS FOR FATHER AND SON
Frank Lampard and Frank Lampard Jr are two of the biggest names at the club. Frank Snr is the assistant boss and spent almost all of his career as a player at the club, making 660 appearances as a full-back. His son is all set for an even more illustrious career having already captained the England under-21 side and also featuring in the senior squad.

G IS FOR GOALS
West Ham's biggest victory was 10-0 against Bury in a League Cup tie in 1983. Among the goalscorers was Tony Cottee who scored four.

H IS FOR HARRY REDKNAPP
The current West Ham boss, who was also hugely popular as a player at Upton Park about 30 years ago. Last season, Harry took The Hammers to their highest placing in the league (fifth) since the Premiership began in 1992.

I IS for ISRAELI
The nationality of former West Ham star Eyal Berkovic. One of the most talented midfielders to play for the club in recent years, the tricky little player joined from Southampton in 1997.

J IS FOR JULES RIMET
The old name for the World Cup, which England won in 1966 at Wembley against West Germany. In the team that day were three legendary West Ham players: captain Bobby Moore, Martin Peters and hat-trick hero Geoff Hurst.

K IS FOR KNIGHTHOOD
An honour received recently by ex-Hammers hero and England hat-trick legend Geoff Hurst for his contribution to the World Cup win. The hat-trick was no fluke, Hurst was a prolific goalscorer throughout his career, and in his 499 appearances for West Ham, he scored 248 goals.

L IS FOR LIST
United's list of trophies reads: FA Cup: 1964, 1975 and 1980, and Cup Winners' Cup: 1965.

A

D

F

WEST HAM

A HISTORY OF THE UPTON PARK HAMMERS – FROM A TO Z!

M IS FOR MONEY
When West Ham sold striker John Hartson to Wimbledon in February 1999, they received £7.5 million in return, a club record for an outgoing player.

N IS FOR 95 years
The length of time it has been since West Ham moved to the Boleyn Ground at Upton Park. The club's only previous home was further east at Canning Town.

O IS FOR OWN SONG
The most famous tune heard from the stands at Upton Park is the cockney favourite 'I'm Forever Blowing Bubbles', which has been a terrace favourite for Hammers fans since anyone can remember.

P IS FOR PREVIOUS NAME
United's original name was Thames Ironworks FC, which they were known as between 1895 and 1900. It explains where one of the teams less used nicknames – The Irons – comes from.

Q IS FOR QUICK
Rio Ferdinand, still aged only 20, is regarded as one of the speediest defenders in the Premiership, an attribute that gave him his first England cap at the age of 19 against Cameroon. Since then he's become a regular in the senior squad.

R IS FOR RED CARDS
At the end of the 1998/99 season, three West Ham players had the misfortune to see red in the same game, at home to Leeds. The list of shame reads Ian Wright, Shaka Hislop and Steve Lomas.

S IS FOR SPORTS COUNCIL
An organisation headed by former Upton Park favourite and well-known BBC pundit, Trevor Brooking. He capped his long West Ham career with the winning goal in the 1980 FA Cup Final against Arsenal.

T IS FOR TSV MUNICH
The side West Ham beat to secure their one and only European trophy – the Cup Winners' Cup in 1965.

U IS FOR UP-AND COMING YOUNGSTERS
Seveenteen-year-old midfielder Joe Cole has been described as the most naturally gifted player to emerge in England since Paul Gascoigne. He was part of the West Ham youth side that won the FA Youth Cup and Championship play-off in 1999.

V IS FOR VICTORIES
Spurred on by their FA Cup success, West Ham went on to clinch the Second Division title in 1980/81 in stylish fashion – setting a new club record of victories in a season by winning 28 out of their 42 games.

W IS FOR WHITE HORSE FINAL
The name used to describe the first ever FA Cup Final at Wembley in 1923 when 127,000 people crammed into the stadium to see the game between Bolton and West Ham. There were so many fans inside the ground that they spilled onto the pitch and wouldn't budge until a white police horse called Billy led the charge to clear the area. Sadly, West Ham lost the game 2-0.

X IS FOR XMAS
The Christmas of 1963 was not a happy one for The Hammers. They suffered their worst ever defeat on Boxing Day 1963, 8-2 at the hands of Blackburn.

Y IS FOR YOUNGEST PLAYER
The Hammers' Paul Allen became the youngest star to appear in an FA Cup Final in 1980, aged 17 years and 256 days. West Ham beat Arsenal at Wembley 1-0.

Z IS FOR ZERO
The number of lower division sides that have managed to win the FA Cup since West Ham did so in 1980, while they were in the old Second Division.

FAMOUS WINS
CELTIC

The Celtic faithful in full voice as their team take Glasgow rivals Rangers apart.

TEAMS
CELTIC v RANGERS

MATCH
SCOTTISH PREMIER LEAGUE

VENUE
CELTIC PARK

DATE
NOVEMBER 22, 1998

STORY

Rangers might have won a Scottish treble of trophies last season but it still didn't stop their Glasgow rivals from notching their biggest Old Firm win in 32 years. Star of the show was Celtic new boy Lubomir Moravcik who scored the goals which had put Celtic two ahead after 49 minutes. The Bhoys' Swedish hero, Henrik Larsson, weighed in with two of his own, while youngster Mark Burchill completed the rout a minute before the end. Giovanni Van Bronckhurst bagged Rangers' only goal of the game but it wasn't enough to spare their blushes.

FINAL SCORE
CELTIC 5 RANGERS 1

Celtic's Phil O'Donnell races for the ball ahead of Rangers striker Rod Wallace.

Henrik Larsson celebrates his two-goal salvo against Rangers.

Larsson outjumps Rangers' Arthur Numan to head Celtic's fourth goal.

The Bhoys go one up and it's time to celebrate!

Celtic go into a huddle before the game begins – whatever they said it certainly did the trick!

DAVID BECKHAM
MAN UNITED

They don't come any bigger than United star Becks, the finest crosser of a ball in England, if not Europe. He can blast it in, bend it round or score from mind-boggling distances! No wonder England boss Kevin Keegan once said that if scientists ever started to clone footballers Becks should be the first into the lab. A nice idea Kev, but we all know that there's only one David Beckham.

YOUNG RED

Despite being born in Leytonstone, east London, David was a major Man United fan right from the start. While winning a heap of footie trophies as a schoolboy he dreamed of playing for The Red Devils at Old Trafford. Little did he know what the future would hold...

UNITED FIRED INTO FINAL

Following a loan spell with Preston in '95 Becks returns to Old Trafford and becomes an important member of the United team alongside Eric Cantona and Ryan Giggs. United take the league title but it's the boy Beckham who fires them into the FA Cup Final with a winner against Chelsea. A Cantona goal clinches the double at Wembley.

COOL ON THE CATWALK

When he isn't showing off his footie skills Becks isn't adverse to a bit of modelling. Just check out this floppy fringed pose from 1998. The Beckham Boy looks like he hasn't got a care in the world, but France '98 is just aroun the corner and the David Beckham story is about to take a few more 'interesting' twists.

THE STATS

- **SUPPORTS** MAN UNITED
- **BORN** LONDON 2/5/75
- **HEIGHT** 6ft
- **WEIGHT** 11st 9lbs
- **TEAMS** MAN UNITED (1992-PRESENT); PRESTON (LOAN 1995)
- **INTERNATIONAL STATUS** FULL ENGLAND INTERNATIONAL – DEBUT v MOLDOVA, SEPTEMBER 1996

THE YOUNG PLAYER OF THE YEAR

To wrap up a marvellous domestic season for Beckham it's little surprise when he is named Young Player Of The Year 1997 by the Professional Footballers' Association. He's the first United star to lift the trophy since Ryan Giggs in 1993.

FREE-KICK MAGIC

England start their World Cu campaign poorly and desperat need to beat Colombia to adva to the next stage. Up steps Be who thumps a beautiful free-k past the South Americans' stranded 'keeper to seal a priceless 2-0 win.

Sh✷ot

3

WIMBLEDON WONDER GOAL

On the first day of the 1996/97 season Becks really puts himself on the map. United are 2-0 up against Wimbledon and Becks receives the ball out near the half-way line. Spotting Dons 'keeper Neil Sullivan off his line, Becks has a shot. It sails over Sully's head into the back of the net. Classic!

AN ENGLAND CAREER BLOSSOMS

Becks made his England debut in September 1996 in a World Cup qualifier against Moldova. England won the game 3-0 and Becks found himself a regular in the team under Glenn Hoddle. He was also part of the famous side which clinched a place at France '98 by holding Italy to a 0-0 draw in Rome in 1997.

4

8

DISASTER!

England and Becks' France '98 campaign comes to a juddering stop against Argentina. Beckham is red carded in the second half for kicking out at Diego Simeone, whose play acting isn't punished at all. Down to ten men England bravely hold the Argies at bay through the rest of the match and into extra-time. Sadly, they lose the game on penalties.

9

A SPICEY ENGAGEMENT

It's not all bad news for Becks. Most of the country might blame him for England's World Cup exit but there's at least one person who still believes in him – his girlfriend Victoria Adams (aka Posh Spice). The two announce their engagement amidst a blaze of publicity.

IN THE FIRING LINE

United's first away game of the 1998/99 season takes them to Upton Park. Still furious with Becks for his World Cup red card West Ham's supporters give him nothing but abuse for 90 minutes. It's the tip of the iceberg as the young United star becomes UK football's public enemy NO.1.

10

DAVID BECKHAM

BACK TO BUSINESS

Trying to put the past behind him Becks gets back to what he does best – scoring great goals. As United's Champions League campaign gathers steam they share a six-goal thriller with Spanish giants Barcelona at the Nou Camp. Becks get on the scoresheet with one of his special swerving, curving free-kicks!

11

12

MEET BROOKLYN BECKHAM

As United chase trophies on three fronts there's more good news for Becks and Posh – the arrival of a baby boy. They name him Brooklyn and the proud dad even has his name tattooed on his back as a tribute! adidas then go even further by presenting Becks with a pair of boots which also feature the little lad's name!

13

A DAZZLING DOUBLE

United put a poor 1998 behind them by claiming their third league and FA Cup double in five years in 1999. Despite transfer speculation linking him with a move to London Becks tells the press that he wants to remain at Old Trafford for life. Many fans and pundits reckon he should be named Player Of The Year ahead of David Ginola.

14

HISTORY'S GREATEST TEAM?

Even after clinching the double United aren't satisfied. They go to Barcelona to face Bayern Munich in the Champions League Final and are 1-0 down with just a minute or two left in injury time. Last gasp goals by substitutes Ole Solskjaer and Teddy Sheringham spark a miraculous comeback and United are champions of Europe. Becks and the boys have won the flippin' lot!

Shoot

DAVID BECKHAM

MAN UNITED

PAST
CHRIS WADDLE

Geordie Chris returned to the English game in style in 1992 after three years at French side Marseille. The former Newcastle and Tottenham star spent four seasons at Wednesday in which his dazzling wing play established him as one of the finest players ever to grace the Hillsborough turf.

a hero from hillsborough's past, another from its present and a whizz-kid to watch in the future.

PRESENT
WIM JONK

Dutch playmaker Jonk showed glimpses of his creative greatness last term in what was a disappointing season for Wednesday. Fans will be hoping this campaign sees the 32-year-old recapture the sparkling form he showed for Holland during France '98. When Jonk fires on all cylinders he can be one of the most creative players in the country, and Boss Danny Wilson will be looking to his £2.5 million signing to inspire The Owls to something better than their customary mid-table obscurity.

FUTURE

MARK McKEEVER

The Derry-born 20-year-old left-wing wizard made his full debut against Chelsea last season, after impressing in loan spells at Bristol Rovers and Reading. The young Irishman has also established himself as a Repubic Of Ireland under-21 international, and Ireland boss Mick McCarthy will be keeping a watchful eye as Euro 2000 approaches. Petter Rudi may find himself warming the bench this season if young McKeever continues his progress.

FUTURE
WEDNESDAY

A TO Z

NIL SATIS NISI OPTI[MUM]

E IS FOR ESCAPE
Everton are regarded as the Premiership's Houdini club, having avoided the drop twice on the last day of the season in recent years. In 1993, they came from 2-0 down to beat Wimbledon 4-2, while in 1998, a draw at home to Coventry was enough to see them safe.

F IS FOR FIXTURE CONGESTION
Players nowadays complain that they have to play too many games, but nothing can compare to the fixture congestion of the 1980s when there were 22 teams in the top-flight. Two seasons in a row, between 1984 and 1986, Everton played 63 games in all competitions.

G IS FOR GREATEST GOALSCORER EVER
Everton legend Dixie Dean is probably the best marksman English football has known. Between 1925 and 1937, the man from Birkenhead scored 377 goals for Everton in 431 games, including 60 goals in 39 league games in the 1927/28 title-winning season.

H IS FOR HONOURS
Everton are one of the most successful clubs in England and have won no less than nine league titles, five FA Cups and the European Cup Winners' Cup in 1985, when they beat Rapid Vienna 3-1.

I IS FOR INCARCERATED
Striker Duncan Ferguson was a Goodison Park favourite between 1994-98. He was best known for two things: firstly, that he kept pigeons, and secondly, that he was once imprisoned for assaulting another player while at Rangers.

J IS FOR JUNIOR PLAYERS
Everton have an excellent youth policy which has seen the likes of Francis Jeffers, Michael Ball, Michael Branch, Richard Dunne and Danny Cadamarteri graduate to the Goodison Park first team in the last couple of years.

K IS FOR Howard KENDALL
Popular as a Toffees midfielder in the late '60s and early '70s, Kendall returned to the club as boss in 1981 and guided them to FA Cup glory against Watford in 1984. The following year the club won the league and Cup Winners' Cup.

L IS FOR LOCAL RIVALS
One of the great local derbies in the English game is Liverpool v Everton. The two Merseyside clubs first played each other in 1894 and have squared up at Wembley twice in FA Cup finals. Unfortunately, Everton lost both.

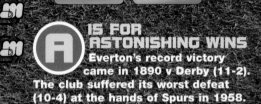

A IS FOR ASTONISHING WINS
Everton's record victory came in 1890 v Derby (11-2). The club suffered its worst defeat (10-4) at the hands of Spurs in 1958.

B IS FOR BRIBES
In 1964, Everton skipper Tony Kay was accused of accepting bribes to throw a match in his time at Sheff Wed. Kay never played for Everton again and was eventually sent to prison.

C IS FOR CLEAN SHEETS
Everton hold a rare record of reaching an FA Cup Final without conceding a goal. The Toffees managed to win the final too – against Sheffield Wednesday – 3-2.

D IS FOR DUSTMAN
The one-time occupation of ex-'keeper Neville Southall. Big Nev holds the record for all-time Everton appearances (750 – 566 in the league) and he was capped 92 times by Wales.

EVERTON

M IS FOR MOONLIGHT DRIBBLERS
Everton's nickname in their very early days. Apparently the team used to train at night using the moon to light up their sessions.

N IS FOR previous NAME
The club was known as St Domingos when it was formed in 1878, after a church sunday school of the same name. They became Everton a year later.

O IS FOR ONE SEASON WONDER
In 1985 Gary Lineker joined Everton, but only spent one season on Merseyside. However, the 1986 World Cup Golden Boot winner didn't pick up any winners' medals that year, despite netting 38 times for the club. After his World Cup success, Lineker opted to join Barcelona where Terry Venables was manager.

P IS FOR PROUD SKIPPER
Kevin Ratcliffe became one of the youngest captains to lift the FA Cup when Everton won it in 1984. The defender went on to play 461 times for the club.

Q IS FOR QUEEN VICTORIA
She was on the throne when Everton joined 11 other professional clubs and formed the Football League in 1888. The Toffees have since been relegated just twice.

R IS FOR Joe ROYLE
The former Everton boss who enjoyed happier times at the club as a player. He still holds the record for being the youngest ever player to don the blue shirt, making his debut in January 1966, aged 16 years, 288 days. He scored 119 times in 275 games.

S IS FOR STANLEY PARK
The great green divide which separates Anfield from Goodison Park. It was also The Toffees' home between 1878 and 1882. Goodison is situated on the north edge of the park and has been Everton's home since 1892.

T IS FOR TV PUNDIT
Sky Sports presenter Andy Gray was hugely popular in his time at Everton in the 1980s. A brave forward, he scored 22 times in 68 games, including in the 1984 FA Cup Final and 1985 Cup Winners' Cup Final.

U IS FOR UNBEATEN RUN
The longest the club has gone without losing a league game is 28 matches, achieved in the title winning season of 1984/85.

V IS FOR VETERAN
Dave Watson, the Everton skipper, who has turned out almost 500 times since joining the club in 1986, forming a solid defensive partnership with Kevin Ratcliffe and winning a Championship medal in his first season.

W IS FOR WORLD CUP VENUE
Goodison was a major venue during the 1966 World Cup, hosting five games in all, including England's 1-1 draw with Brazil.

X IS FOR X-FACTOR
Or unknown number. In the 1933 FA Cup Final Everton made counting the number of players on the pitch easier for referees by becoming the first club to put the numbers 1-11 on the back of players' shirts.

Y IS FOR YE ANCIENT EVERTON TOFFEE HOUSE
The name of the hotel which was situated near where the original Everton club played, and the origin of the club's nickname, The Toffees.

Z IS FOR ZENITH DATA SYSTEMS CUP.
Everton got to the Final of this ill-fated competition in 1990. Unfortunately, They lost 4-1 to Crystal Palace.

O

P

FAMOUS WINS
COVENTRY

TEAM
ASTON VILLA v COVENTRY

MATCH
FA CUP FIFTH ROUND

VENUE
VILLA PARK

DATE
FEBRUARY 14, 1998

STORY

Coventry hadn't beaten Aston Villa at Villa Park for 62 years before this midlands cup derby. But Gordon Strachan's men broke the spell thanks to a winner from sub Viorel Moldovan in the 72nd minute. Moldovan became The Sky Blues' biggest ever signing when they snapped him up from Grasshoppers Of Zurich for £3.25 million in December 1997. Sadly for the Romanian the goal proved to be the highlight of his short-lived Highfield Road career. Unable to find his goalscoring form he was sold to Turkish side Fenerbahce just seven months after joining.

FINAL SCORE
VILLA 0 COVENTRY 1

Villa striker Stan Collymore under pressure from Coventry midfielder Roland Nilsson.

Viorel Moldovan celebrates his one and only great moment in a Coventry shirt!

Julian Joachim legs it past Roland Nilsson but Coventry hang on for their famous win.

Coventry recorded their first win at Villa Park in 62 years – and there was nothing Julian Joachim could do about it.

Coventry boss Gordon Strachan congratulates his goal scorer at the end of the game.

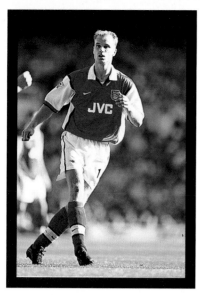

DENNIS BERGKAMP
ARSENAL

The complete player. One foot is as amazing as the other and like a chess grandmaster he's always six moves ahead of the opposition. He joined Arsenal in 1995 after two miserable seasons in Italy with Inter Milan. He cost The Gunners £7.5 million but has repaid that fee time and again with his skillful displays and breathtaking goals. Bergkamp is arguably the most successful foreign signing of all time.

THE STATS

- ✪ **SUPPORTS** TOTTENHAM
- ✪ **BORN** AMSTERDAM 18/5/69
- ✪ **HEIGHT** 6ft
- ✪ **WEIGHT** 12st 5lbs
- ✪ **TEAMS** AJAX (1986-93); INTER MILAN (1993-95); ARSENAL (1995-PRESENT)
- ✪ **INTERNATIONAL STATUS** FULL HOLLAND INTERNATIONAL – DEBUT v ITALY, SEPTEMBER 1990

AJAX ACE

Bergy was a product of the famous youth academy at Ajax. He made his debut for the famous Dutch team in December 1986 and ended up helping them to a league title (1990), two Dutch cups ('87 and '93), a Cup Winners' Cup ('87) and the UEFA Cup ('92). A successful start!

DENNIS SINKS THE SCOTS

Holland make it to the Finals of the European Championships in Sweden in 1992. Bergy announces his presence to the world with a goal against Scotland. The Dutch are eventually eliminated on penalties by Denmark in the Semis.

HIGHBURY BOUND

Arsenal boss Bruce Rioch snaps Bergy up for £7.5 million from Inter Milan in the summer of 1995. The Dutchman makes his Gunners debut against Middlesbrough on August 20, but fails to get on the scoresheet as his new team scrape a 1-1 draw.

BERGY'S BRACE

Six games in to the season Dennis is still without a goal. That changes in the match v Southampton at Highbury. He scores twice as The Gunners win 4-2. The maestro announces his arrival.

ENGLAND v HOLLAND

Euro '96 in England is probably a tournament Bergy would like to forget. The Dutch struggle and get blown away by England who beat them 4-1. Holland are eventually eliminated from the tournament altogether by France, 5-4 on penalties in the Quarter-Finals.

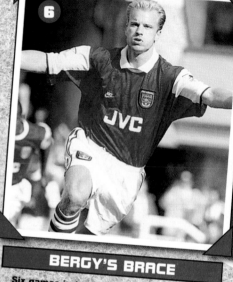

JEEZ, IT'S THE CHEESE!

He might be a highly-paid footie professional but Dennis still likes a laugh. Here he is in an ad for a sportswear company wondering what he might have done with his life had he not been a footie star – worked in cheese factory by the looks of it!

Shoot

BERGY BLOWS IT IN ITALY

3 Dennis moves to Italian giants Inter Milan in 1993 but finds it tough going in Serie A. He scores just 11 times in 52 appearances and although he's part of the team which lifts the UEFA Cup in 1994, rumours linking him with a move to England start to surface regularly in the newspapers.

AMERICAN DREAM

4 Bergkamp's first World Cup (USA '94) is a successful one for him but less so for Holland. The Dutch crash out in the Quarter-Finals to eventual winners Brazil but Dennis The Menace plays a blinder, scoring three of his team's eight goals during the tournament. Still, his future in Italy remains uncertain.

ARSENAL GUN 'EM ALL DOWN!

10 Dennis's amazing season is complete as The Gunners achieve the second League and Cup double in their history. Arsenal pip Man United to the title by a point and breeze past Newcastle at Wembley to claim the FA Cup. Their run of form includes beating The Red Devils home and away in the Premiership and trouncing them in the following season's Charity Shield at Wembley.

9 PLAYER POWER!

With Arsenal going well in the Premiership and FA Cup, it's little surprise when Dennis receives both Player Of The Year awards for 1998. Bergy finishes the season as the club's top league scorer with 16 goals. But his individual achievements pale in comparison to what Arsenal achieve as a team...

DENNIS BERGKAMP ARSENAL

11

MICHAEL WHO?

Holland quickly progress to the Quarter-Finals of France '98, where Bergkamp scores a goal against Argentina every bit as good Michael Owen's crowd stopper versus the same team. Bringing the ball down, Bergy flicks it behind a static Argentine defender, before curling it past 'keeper Carlos Roa.

12

PAIN OF THE PENALTIES

Holland go into the Semi-Finals against Brazil and are trailing until the 87th minute when Patrick Kluivert's strike throws them a life-line. Sadly for the Dutch, it isn't enough. The scores remain 1-1 after extra-time and Holland are eliminated 4-2 on penalties, although Dennis scores his spot-kick.

13

EUROPEAN HOPES FADE

Arsenal's Champions League campaign is hampered by injury and Bergkamp's fear of flying. But Dennis does what he can in Arsenal's home ties at Wembley, heading Lee Dixon's cross into the net to give The Gunners the lead against Dinamo Kiev. It isn't enough though and they bow out at the group stage.

14

POTLESS GUNNERS

Arsenal's 1998/99 season ends badly. They fail to retain their League title despite winning the same number of points as in their Double season. Bergy also misses a last minute penalty in the FA Cup Semi-Final against Man United, who go on to win the tie and the trophy.

DENNIS
BERGKAMP

ARSENAL

Before Clough's amazing managerial career most notably with Nott'm Forest, he was one of the most feared strikers in the land. In his playing days during the late 1950s and early '60s he succeeded in notching up a mind boggling 251 strikes in just 274 games for Sunderland and Middlesbrough. He also claimed a pair of England caps before a crippling knee injury cut short his goalscoring antics at the age of 28.

Shoot presents a Mackems legend from the past, a hero from the present and one to watch for the future.

PRESENT
KEVIN PHILLIPS

Gaffer Peter Reid will be hoping that England star Phillips can continue his goal grabbing form as Sunderland look to consolidate their position as a top-flight club. The former Watford man overcame a serious toe injury last season, and despite a four month lay off still managed to bag 24 goals to go with the 35 he scored the previous season.

PAST PRESENT SUNDE

MICHAEL BRIDGES

The 21-year-old striker is one of the hottest properties in the game. On his Sunderland debut as a 17-year-old in 1996 he scored within 12 seconds of coming on as a sub against Southend. The England under-21 star struggled with injury last term but still managed to hit 12 goals in the first half of the season.

A TO Z

M.C.F.C.

Superbia In Proelio

A IS FOR ATTENDANCE
As in City's highest, which was 84,569 for an FA Cup Quarter-Final against Stoke in 1934. When Maine Road was opened in 1923, it was the second biggest ground in the country after Wembley.

B IS FOR inflatable BANANAS
Which were famous on the terraces wherever City fans stood around the country in the late 1980s. The origins of this craze are unknown, but it soon sparked a trend copied by other fans.

C IS FOR CHELSEA
The team which beat City in the Final of the Full Member's Cup at Wembley in 1986. The score was 5-4!

D IS FOR DIVISION TWO
Where City found themselves for the first time ever in 1998 after one of the most disastrous season's in the club's history.

E IS FOR EVERTON
The Toffees inflicted a 9-1 defeat on The Blues, their worst ever, in Sept. 1906.

F IS FOR FUTCHER
The surname of the only pair of twins to play for the club. Ron and Paul were Maine Road stars in the late '70s. Ron played upfront, while brother Paul slotted in at the back.

G IS FOR GEORGIAN
The nationality of one of the club's best-known players of recent years, Georgiou Kinkladze. He joined the club in 1995 and was sold for a club record £5 million to Ajax in 1998.

H IS FOR HALLOWED TURF OF WEMBLEY
Where City won promotion back to the First Division in the Play-Off Final last May. They beat Gillingham 3-1 on penalties after grabbing a draw with two late goals.

I IS FOR INTERNATIONALS
Keith Curle, the former City captain, was the last Maine Road star to play for England, the last of his three caps coming in 1993 under Graham Taylor. The most capped player at the club was England international Colin Bell who won 48 caps between 1968 and 1976.

J IS FOR JOYOUS TIMES
Such as the late 1960s when City won the League in 1968, the FA Cup in 1969 and the League Cup and Cup Winners' Cup in 1970.

K IS FOR KIPPAX
The name of a large area of terracing at Maine Road, famous for creating the ground's famous noisy atmosphere. It was demolished in the mid-'90s, following the Taylor Report, which effectively banned terracing after the Hillsborough disaster.

L IS FOR Denis LAW
The City star who had previously enjoyed a hugely successful career at rivals Manchester United. He even helped condemn his former side to relegation in 1974 by scoring against them with a cheeky backheel!

M IS FOR MOON
As in Blue Moon, the club's unofficial theme song. It was originally a rock 'n' roll hit back in the 1950s.

N IS FOR NONSENSE
A good word to describe some of the crazy things that have happened to City in the past decade. From beating Man United 5-1 in 1990 and finishing fifth in the top flight in 1991 and 1992, the club

G H

Nationwide
FF WINNERS

K

MAN CITY

A HISTORY OF THE MAINE ROAD SIDE FROM A-Z!

suffered an unstoppable slide which saw them relegated from the Premiership in 1996 and relegated again two years later to Division Two. Between 1995 and 1996, the club had five different managers, including Steve Coppell who lasted just six games before quitting!

O IS FOR Alan OAKES
He holds the record for the most appearances in a City shirt. He played 565 times for the Maine Road club between 1959 and 1976.

P IS FOR PRISONER OF WAR
Which is what legendary German 'keeper Bert Trautmann was during World War Two. He stayed on in England when the war was over, going to Maine Road in 1949. He played a total of 545 games for the club, including the 1956 FA Cup win over Birmingham, in which he broke his neck but carried on playing!

Q IS FOR QUALITY
Young striker Terry Cooke had a massive impact after arriving at Maine Road from Man United. His goals helped put the club into the Play-Off Final.

R IS FOR Joe ROYLE
The current City manager who didn't arrive in time to stop the club sliding into Division Two in 1998. Since then, however, the former Everton boss has built a new, improved side which bounced back into Division One at the first attempt.

S IS FOR penalty SAVES
Young City 'keeper, Nicky Weaver, became an instant Wembley hero after he saved two penalties during his club's Play-Off Final win over Gillingham last May.

T IS FOR TWENTY EIGHT THOUSAND
Which was the approximate average attendance for City's Division Two home games in the 1998/99 season. There are Premiership teams which would kill for that kind of fan loyalty!

U IS FOR UNITED
City's hated rivals, Manchester United, who have had their most successful period in history, while City have just recovered from their worst.

V IS FOR VACATING
City are set to leave their famous Maine Road ground in the next few years to move to a brand new, state-of-the-art stadium which is currently being built for the 2002 Commonwealth Games. City have been resident at Maine Road since 1923.

W IS FOR WINNERS
City have won nine major trophies in their history, including two League titles and four FA Cups. Their last League Championship triumph was way back in 1968, while their last FA Cup victory came in 1969 when they beat Leciester 1-0.

X IS FOR A DRAW ON THE POOLS COUPON
In the 1993/94 season, City set a new club record by drawing a massive 18 of their 42 Premier League matches. They only won nine league games all season and were probably lucky to finish 16th.

Y IS FOR YESTERYEAR
When the cream of British talent played for a flamboyant and successful City side. Names such as Rodney Marsh, Denis Law, Mike Summerbee and Neil Young are among the greats who regularly graced Maine Road with their skills in the '60s and '70s.

Z IS FOR Gornik ZABRZE
In 1970 Man City became the third English club to lift the European Cup Winners' Cup after beating Hungarian side Gornik Zabrze 2-1, in Vienna, in front of just 10,000 supporters. It remains City's only success in Europe.

FAMOUS WINS
QUEENS PARK

TEAMS
MAN UNITED v QPR

MATCH
DIVISION ONE FIXTURE

VENUE
OLD TRAFFORD

DATE
JANUARY 1, 1992

STORY

A freak league result on New Year's Day 1992 in which a little remembered QPR striker by the name of Dennis Bailey ran riot against a Man United side who were then top of the league and had lost just once all season. United were two down at half-time thanks to goals from Andy Sinton and Bailey's first, but the player nicknamed The Rev (because of his Christian beliefs) went on to shock the 38,554 gathered at Old Trafford with a second half brace. Bailey now plays for Colchester in case you are wondering.

FINAL SCORE
MAN UNITED 1 QPR 4

Rangers' players celebrate their famous victory over Alex Ferguson's United stars.

All praise The Rev: QPR's Dennis Bailey, now at Colchester.

RANGERS

Dennis Bailey celebrates his Old Trafford hat-trick as Peter Schmeichel and The Red Devils are shocked by QPR.

Gary Pallister and Paul Ince try to put the squeeze on QPR hat-trick hero Dennis Bailey.

SOL CAMPBELL
TOTTENHAM

Solid at the back, quicker than a bullet on the counter-attack, that's Tottenham & England man mountain Sol Campbell. The London-born central defender made his bow for Spurs in December 1992 as a sub in the Premiership clash with Chelsea. Although the White Hart Lane outfit lost that day, Campbell got himself on the scoresheet and hasn't looked back since. And at 25 years old his best days are still in front of him.

⚽ THE STATS

- ⚪ **SUPPORTS TOTTENHAM**
- ⚪ **BORN LONDON 18/9/74**
- ⚪ **HEIGHT 6ft 2ins**
- ⚪ **WEIGHT 14st 4lbs**
- ⚪ **TEAMS TOTTENHAM (1992-PRESENT)**
- ⚪ **INTERNATIONAL STATUS FULL ENGLAND INTERNATIONAL – DEBUT v HUNGARY, MAY 1996**

1 EARLY DAYS

A Tottenham boy from day one, Sol tasted success at an early age as the Spurs youth side won their version of the League Cup. He is quickly recognised as a born leader and an excellent reader of the game. Expect this boy to go far!

SOL'S SPURS DEBUT

Sol makes his Tottenham first team debut against Chelsea at Stamford Bridge as a substitute on December 5, 1992. Spurs lose the game 2-1 but Sol scores his side's goal. His reward? He doesn't make another first team appearance all season and doesn't return to the side until the following August. He's very much a regular after that though.

THE GREAT WALL

Terry Venables whisks his England squad off for a tour of the far east as part of his Euro '96 preparations. England beat China and a Hong Kong select side and Sol gets another run out in the latter game. He also checks out the Great Wall Of China, a massive obstacle which keeps out the opposition – just like Sol!

7 THE BIG TIME

England make the Semi-Finals of Euro '96 after beating Spain at Wembley on penalties (pictured). Sol makes just one appearance – as an 84th minute sub in the 2-0 win over Scotland, but his international future seems assured.

5 GONE GOLFIN'

With hardly any breathing space between the end of the season and Euro '96 starting, Sol has to take every chance he can to take it easy. Here he is indulging in most footy stars' fave pastime – golf!

Shoot

3

EUROPEAN SUCCESS

Sol's trophy cabinet is already filling up, as he helps England to under-18 glory in the European Championships during the summer of 1993. He's pictured here with international team-mates Chris Day (left) and Darren Caskey, who were also Tottenham trainees.

4

SOL THE ENGLAND MAN!

Sol's excellent form for his club side inevitably leads to a full England call up. Sol makes his senior international debut against Hungary in a Wembley friendly just prior to Euro '96. It's a good day for Campbell and Terry Venables' men as they run out comfortable 3-0 winners – Sol makes the European Championship squad too!

8

LIONS ROAR IN ROME

Sol is one of the stars as England hold Italy to a 0-0 draw in Rome in October 1997 under Glenn Hoddle. The result means that England qualify for the following year's World Cup Finals in France and that Italy have to play-off for a place. The entire team put in a truly battling display with young Sol the choice of many as Man Of The Match.

9

SOL SINKS THE ARGIES... NEARLY!

With England v Argentina poised at 2-2 with the minutes ticking away Sol heads what he and the entire population of the country think is a winner. Unfortunately, the referee disallows the goal and Glenn Hoddle's boys crash out to the South Americans on penalties.

IT'S CAPTAIN CAMPBELL

Already captain of his club, Sol is given the ultimate compliment by England boss Glenn Hoddle when he is asked to skipper his country. Sol wears the England armband in a Wembley friendly with the Czech Republic towards the end of 1998. England run out 2-0 winners.

10

SOL CAMPBELL

TOTTENHAM

AUDERE EST FACERE

11

DAZED AND CONFUSED

Campbell gets a severe knock to the head during England's Euro 2000 qualifier against Sweden in Stockholm. It isn't the only knock Campbell suffers that night as his team lose 2-1 and eventually see their Euro 2000 dreams further eroded by draws against Bulgaria and then Sweden, in the two sides' Wembley return.

12

HANDBALL HORROR

Tottenham had been well on top in their FA Cup Semi-Final match against Newcastle, and as the game went into extra-time there looked likely to be only one winner. Then, as a cross flew into the Spurs area, Sol jumped and accidentally handled the ball. Newcastle scored and went on to win the game 2-0. Sol is gutted.

14

NEW KIT, NEW SEASON

George Graham's first season in charge at Spurs has seen the club back amongst the silverware. The question is can they take the next step and join the likes of Man United and Arsenal at the very top. If Sol's got anything to do with it they will!

13

WORTHINGTON WINNERS

With new boss George Graham calling the shots, Sol and Tottenham make their first Wembley final in eight years. They beat Leicester 1-0 with a last minute goal and Sol celebrates his first bit of senior silverware.

SOL
CAMPBELL
TOTTENHAM

Shoot presents an Ewood Park legend, a current Rovers hero and a young star to watch in the future.

PAST
COLIN HENDRY

Next to Alan Shearer, Hendry was probably Rovers' most important player during their glory years of 1992-96, an era which saw the club promoted via the play-offs before clinching their first ever Premiership title. A powerful presence in defence and an inspirational leader, Blackburn's loss has definitely been Scottish Champions Rangers' gain.

PAST PRESENT
BLACK

PRESENT
KEITH GILLESPIE

By his own standards the young Northern Ireland star failed to hit the heights form-wise with Rovers last season following his move from Newcastle. However, expect the dashing winger to really find his form this campaign as the Lancashire club try and battle their way back to the Premiership at the first attempt. It won't be easy with the likes of Ipswich, Fulham and Forest breathing down their necks but if Gillespie can recapture some of the form which made him such a hot property at Man United, Rovers should have few problems.

FUTURE
MATT JANSEN

The former Carlisle and Crystal Palace striker joined the sinking Rovers ship too late to save them from relegation last season. But the talented 22-year-old could make a very big impression in Division One this campaign, alongside fellow forward Ashley Ward.

FUTURE
BURN ROVERS

A TO Z

IPSWICH TOWN FOOTBALL CLUB

A IS FOR ALF RAMSEY
The man who took England to World Cup glory in 1966, also guided Ipswich to their only top-flight title in 1962. When Ramsey took over as boss in 1955, the club played in the Third Division.

B IS FOR BRAVE
Terry Butcher was a rock at the heart of the Ipswich defence in the '80s. He came through the ranks at Portman Road, playing his first full season in 1978-79. He eventually became captain and made his England debut in 1980.

C IS FOR CAPTAIN MARVEL
Mick Mills, who played for Ipswich between 1966 and 1982, clocked up a record 741 appearances as a full-back. During his time at the club, he lifted the FA Cup in 1978 and the UEFA Cup in 1981.

D IS FOR DON'T MENTION THE PLAY-OFFS
Ipswich have reached the play-offs four times since they were introduced in 1987, but have failed to even make it to the final on any of those four occasions.

E IS FOR EUROPEAN SUCCESS
It came in the UEFA Cup in 1981. Midfielder John Wark set a new record for top goalscorer in the competition by netting 14 goals on Town's road to glory which culminated in a 5-4 aggregate final win against AZ67 Alkmaar.

F IS FOR FOREIGN IMPORTS
Two of the most successful players to make it in England during the '80s were Dutch duo Arnold Muhren and Frans Thijssen. The duo became the bedrock of the Ipswich midfield for four successful years, culminating in their UEFA Cup win.

G IS FOR GOALIE
Richard Wright, 22, has established himself as a regular in the England squad after an inspired couple of seasons in the green jersey at Portman Road.

H IS FOR HATED RIVALS
Fortunately Ipswich have the upper hand over their derby opponents Norwich City. They've only lost around a third of their encounters with the boys from Carrow Road.

I IS FOR INTERESTING FACT
A game in 1926 had to be abandoned when rats were discovered in the Main Stand at Portman Road. It wasn't surprising, the groundsman was keeping sheep, goats and chickens in various parts of the ground!

J IS FOR JOHN WARK
Despite playing in midfield, John Wark is Town's third highest scorer of all time. He hit 182 goals in just under 700 games for the club in the '70s and '80s.

K IS FOR KIERON DYER
One of the best home-grown players to emerge from the youth ranks at Portman Road, midfielder Dyer is an England under-21 regular and has played in a variety of roles for both club and country.

L IS FOR LOYAL SKIPPER
Micky Stockwell, the club's current captain has never played for another side, has been a Town regular since 1982 and has made well over 500 appearances for the club.

M IS FOR MANAGERIAL SUCCESS
While Alf Ramsey brought the league title to Portman Road,

C

E

Work for MANPOWER for Work

F

IPSWICH ★★★★★

A HISTORY OF THE BLUES THAT'S AS EASY AS A-B-C!

Bobby Robson won the FA Cup (1978) and the UEFA Cup (1981) while he was in charge. Like Ramsey, Robson's success was noted by the FA who appointed him England boss in 1982.

N IS FOR NEWCOMERS
Ipswich's membership of the Football League is relatively short, having only joined in 1938. The club was formed in the local Town Hall in 1878 when a local MP was made club president.

O IS FOR Roger OSBORNE
The goalscoring hero of the 1978 Cup Final against Arsenal. A left foot strike in the 77th minute ensured his place in Portman Road history forever.

P IS FOR PENALTY SAVING EXPERT
Paul Cooper, a regular between the sticks at Portman Road between 1974 and 1987, was renowned for his brilliant saves from spot-kicks. Cooper spent a great deal of time swotting up on team penalty-takers and working out the likely direction of their kicks. Among those he stopped were Liam Brady, Terry McDermott and Mickey Thomas.

Q IS FOR QUARTER FINAL
When Ipswich met Leeds in the FA Cup Quarter-Final in 1975, it was the first time The Blues had reached that stage of the competition. Not surprising then that a record crowd, 38,010, watched it.

R IS FOR RECORD GOALSCORER
Ray Crawford netted 228 goals in 354 games during his time at the club in the '50s and '60s. During Town's title-winning season, he scored 40 of their 100 league goals, including three hat-tricks.

S IS FOR SCOTTISH MANAGER
George Burley, the current Town boss, took over at the club in 1994. Burley had an illustrious career at Portman Road as a player, making exactly 500 appearances between 1973 and 1985.

T IS FOR THRASHING
The only way to describe the club's biggest win – 10-0 – during a European Cup preliminary match against Maltese side Floriana in September 1962.

U IS FOR UNDEFEATED
Ipswich's longest home unbeaten run ran from October 1979 to March 1981, lasting 33 games in all.

V IS FOR VICTORIES IN A SEASON
When Ipswich finished as runners-up in the top-flight in 1981, they set a new club record by winning 26 games in a season – two more than when they took the title in 1961-62.

W IS FOR WORST SEASON EVER
Ipswich's last season in the top-flight, 1994-95, was their worst ever, with the team only managing seven wins out of 42 games, leaving them bottom of the league.

X IS FOR XMAS
Ipswich played their last ever game on a Christmas Day in 1957 when they held West Ham to a 1-1 draw at Upton Park. Christmas Day fixtures have not been played since.

Y IS FOR YOUNGEST PLAYER
Jason Dozzell became the youngest player to appear in a league game for Town when he came on as a sub for Eric Gates against Coventry City in February 1984 aged just 16 years and 56 days. To cap his day, he scored.

Z IS FOR Romeo ZONDERVAN
The only player to ever appear for Ipswich whose surname starts with Z! Born in Surinam, but raised in Holland, he joined from West Brom in March '94, but returned to Holland in 1992.

K

L

FAMOUS WINS
CHARLTON

TEAMS
CHARLTON v SUNDERLAND

MATCH
DIV ONE PLAY-OFF FINAL

VENUE
WEMBLEY

DATE
MAY 25, 1998

STORY

This Division One Play-Off Final had eight goals (six in 90 minutes, two during extra-time), a hat-trick hero in Charlton's Clive Mendonca and one of the most nerve-wracking penalty shoot-outs in history. The tie was finally settled in The Addicks' favour when their 'keeper, Sasa Ilic, saved Sunderland's seventh penalty from Michael Gray clinching their place in the Premiership for the first time. The irony was that Mendonca had been born and bred in Sunderland and was a life-long Mackems fan!

FINAL SCORE
**CHARLTON 4 SUNDERL'D 4
(CHARLTON WON 7-6 PENS)**

Life-long Sunderland fan Clive Mendonca breaks The Mackems' hearts with Charlton's extra-time equaliser.

After 120 minutes, eight goals and 13 penalties Charlton finally make it to the Premiership. No wonder they're happy!

Sasa Ilic's teammates mob him after the Charlton 'keeper saves Michael Gray's penalty. Ilic is on the bottom of the pile... somewhere!

Charlton's Eddie Youds clears the ball off the line as his team battle for promotion to the Premiership.

GIANFRANCO ZOLA
CHELSEA

Probably Chelsea's most influential and important player of the last few years, Gianfranco Zola was snapped up by The Blues in November 1996 from Parma. The pint-sized Sardinian genius had originally made his name with another Italian side, Napoli, as understudy to the great Diego Maradona. His sublime passing and brilliant free-kicks have made him a fan favourite at Stamford Bridge.

THE STATS

- ⚙ SUPPORTS CHELSEA
- ⚙ BORN OLIENA, ITALY
- ⚙ HEIGHT 5ft 6ins
- ⚙ WEIGHT 10st 10lbs
- ⚙ TEAMS NUORESE (1984-86); TORRES 1987-1989; NAPOLI (1989-1992); PARMA (1992-1997); CHELSEA (1996-PRESENT)
- ⚙ INTERNATIONAL STATUS FULL ITALY INTERNATIONAL – DEBUT v NORWAY, NOVEMBER 1991

1

ON THE MOVE

When Zola joins Napoli in 1989 they are one of Europe's up and coming teams. They'd won the Italian championship for the first time in 1987 and are the UEFA Cup holders. Zola helps them to a second title in 1990, with two goals in 18 appearances.

2

EUROPEAN GLORY

Snapped up by Parma in 1992 Zola wins the European Cup Winners' Cup with them the following year. In the Final at Wembley he leads the Royal Antwerp defence a merry dance as the Italians go on to win 3-1. They make the Final again the following year but are beaten by Arsenal.

5

MORE PENALTY WOE

Italy's terrible luck with penalties continues at Euro '96 in England. The Italians are knocked out of the tournament at the group stage after drawing 0-0 with eventual winners Germany. Zola's seventh minute penalty is saved by German 'keeper Andreas Kopke.

6

HE'S A BLUE

In November 1996, at the age of 30 and out of favour at Parma, Zola joins Ruud Gullit's foreign legion at Chelsea. He becomes the club's third high-profile Italian signing after Gianluca Vialli and Roberto Di Matteo.

7 **ROBIN HOOD**

Dressed up like this you'd think he'd moved to Nott'm Forest not Chelsea! Still, Zola's sharp-shooting proves as accurate as Robin Hood's – he hits 8 goals in 23 league appearances in 1996/97 as Chelsea finish the season 6th.

Shoot

3

WORLD CUP HEARTBREAK

Zola heads out to the United States with the Italian squad for the World Cup in 1994 but it's one he will want to forget. The tiny star is sent off in the 3-2 extra-time win over Nigeria, while Italy themselves are agonisingly defeated on penalties by Brazil in the Final.

4

MORE EURO GLORY

Returning to Italy, Zola and Parma pick up where they left off. They meet fellow Italians Juventus – including young star Alessandro Del Piero (pictured) – in the UEFA Cup Final in 1995 and cause a major upset by defeating them 2-1 over two legs. Juventus had already completed an Italian league and cup double!

8

LIFE IN LONDON

Zola finds settling into his new life easy – after all he's surrounded by Italian-speaking players and west London is one of the country's most salubrious haunts. On the pitch, things go similarly well with Chelsea fast emerging as one of the Premiership's classiest and most exciting teams. But the best is yet to come.

10

FRANCO DESTROYS THE DONS

Chelsea ease through to the FA Cup semi-finals where they meet Wimbledon at Highbury. The game is a one-sided affair with Zola calling all the shots. He scores Chelsea's second in a 3-0 win, turning three defenders on the edge of The Dons' penalty box before coolly pushing the ball past 'keeper Neil Sullivan.

WEMBLY BLISS

With England and Italy battling it out for a place at France '98 the match between the countries at Wembley in February 1997 becomes hugely important. Zola breaks English hearts, however, as he scores the Italians' winner, slotting the ball past Tottenham 'keeper Ian Walker while under pressure from big Sol Campbell.

9

GIANFRANCO ZOLA

CHELSEA

FA CUP WINNER

Zola's first season at Chelsea ended in glory in May 1997 when the club won its first piece of major silverware for 26 years. Their 2-0 FA Cup Final victory over Middlesbrough was particularly notable for a Roberto Di Matteo goal after just 42 seconds into the game – the quickest cup final goal this century.

11

FOOTBALLER OF THE YEAR

An extraordinary season for Franco gets even better when he is named Footballer Of The Year by the Football Writers' Association. He becomes the third foreign star in succession to carry off the award following in the footsteps of Jurgen Klinsmann and Eric Cantona.

12

KINGS OF EUROPE

The following season Chelsea complete a trophy double by winning the League Cup and the European Cup Winners' Cup. A tight, 0-0 draw with Stuttgart is brought to life when substitute Zola takes the field in the second half and scores the winner with only his second touch.

13

A SEASON OF NO SILVERWARE

Despite spending big in the summer manager Gianluca Vialli is unable to guide his team to any silverware during the 1998/99 season. Most upsetting for Zola is The Blues' exit from the Cup Winners' Cup at the Semi-Final stage.

14

Shoot

GIANFRANCO ZOLA
CHELSEA

Shoot presents a Goodison Park legend, a current hero and a young star to watch in the future.

PAST
NEVILLE SOUTHALL

The big Welsh 'keeper reached his peak in the club's glory era of the mid-'80s, being widely acknowledged as the best shot stopper in the world at the time. He was a vital component of The Toffees' sides which won two league titles (1985 and '87) and two FA Cups (1984 and '95) during his 17 years and 578 appearances with the Merseyside club (1981-98).

PAST PRESENT
EVERT

FUTURE
MICHAEL BALL

Cash-strapped Everton boss Walter Smith will have to wheel and deal to hold on to teenage defensive sensation Ball, who many regard as the best young left-back in England. The under-21 international played a vital role in preserving Everton's Premiership status and could be in line for further international honours if he continues his current rate of progress.

PRESENT
DON HUTCHISON

Bought by then Toffees boss Howard Kendall for £1.1 million from Sheffield United in 1997 it was under his successor, Walter Smith, that Hutch broke into the club's first team and really started to blossom. The former Liverpool and West Ham star brought much needed aggression to Everton's light-weight midfield and his battling qualities were undoubtedly one of the main reasons for his side's escape from relegation last season. His form has since earnt him a call up for Scotland.

FUTURE
ON

A TO Z

E **IS FOR ERIC THE RED**
The nickname given to Eric Cantona. Signed from Leeds for a bargain £1 million in 1992, the Frenchman helped the club to their first title for 26 years in 1993. The one year United didn't win the League when Eric was there, was 1995, the season he was banned for nine months for attacking an abusive fan with a kung-fu style kick.

I **IS FOR IPSWICH TOWN**
The unlucky team on the receiving end of United's best ever win. On March 4, 1995 Town got trounced 9-0 at Old Trafford, with Andy Cole scoring five times.

A **IS FOR AWESOME**
A good word to describe Sir Alex Ferguson's record at the club. Since winning his first trophy – the FA Cup in 1990 – United have done the league and cup double twice, plus the treble last season.

F **IS FOR FAMOUS NAMES**
Stars such as David Platt and Peter Beardsley never made the grade at Old Trafford but went on to great success elsewhere. They both played for England in the 1990 World Cup semi-final against West Germany.

J **IS FOR JUVENTUS**
When United beat Juve in Turin on April 21, 1999 it was the first time they'd defeated an Italian side away from home.

B **IS FOR the BIGGEST CROWD**
Old Trafford's highest attendance isn't for a United game at all. 76,962 crammed into the stadium on March 25, 1939 to watch an FA Cup semi-final match.

G **IS FOR GROUNDSHARE**
In 1941, Old Trafford suffered severe bomb damage in a German air attack on Manchester. When the war ended in 1945 and football resumed, United were forced to share Man City's Maine Road ground for four years while their own stadium was repaired.

K **IS FOR KIT**
United came a cropper against Southampton on April 13, 1996 – and blamed the kit they were wearing! Three down at half-time, United complained that their grey away kit was making it hard to see each other and changed into a different blue and white kit. They still went on to lose 3-1!

C **IS FOR Bobby CHARLTON**
The former United skipper and England World Cup winner holds several Old Trafford records, including the most league goals (199) and most league appearances (606). He's also the most capped Man United player with 106 England appearances.

H **IS FOR HUGE HANDS**
Like the ones possessed by Peter Schmeichel, arguably United's best ever 'keeper. He left Old Trafford last summer after eight trophy-filled years.

L **IS FOR LEYTONSTONE**
The east London suburb where David Beckham was born on May 2, 1975. Despite living much nearer White Hart Lane and Upton Park than Old Trafford Becks was a United fan from the word go.

D **IS FOR Red DEVILS**
The club's famous nickname. They've certainly tormented a few opponents over the years!

M **IS FOR MUNICH AIR CRASH**
The worst moment in the club's history came on February 6, 1958 when a plane crash

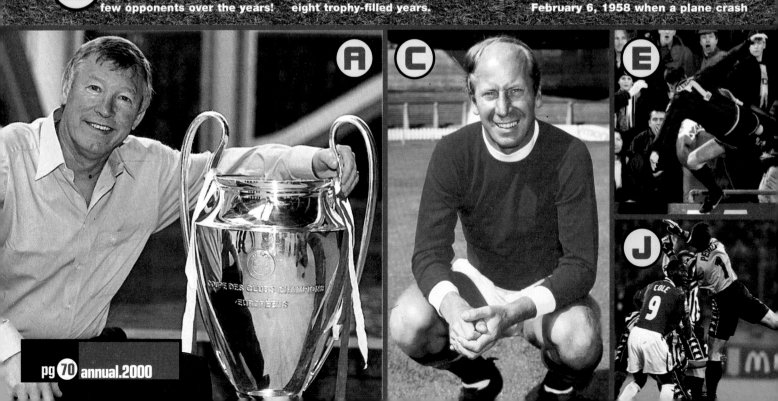

on the runway at Munich airport in Germany claimed the lives of eight United players on board. The team had been returning from Belgrade, where they had clinched a place in the European Cup semi-finals.

N IS FOR NORWAY
Home country of Ole Gunnar Solskjaer, who despite only starting nine games last season, scored 18 goals, including the European Cup Final winner.

O IS FOR ORIGINAL NAME
Newton Heath FC were formed in 1878 and admitted to the Second Division in 1892. The club went bankrupt in 1902 and re-emerged as Manchester United later the same year.

P IS FOR PRODIGY
The late, great Sir Matt Busby built a young side – The Busby Babes – which won the league three times in the 1950s and, before the Munich air crash, was set to conquer Europe. Amazingly, Busby built a new team that went on to league, FA Cup and European Cup success in the 1960s.

Q IS FOR QUEUE
Something United fans must be used to, especially if they're trying to get tickets for games at Old Trafford. In this country alone there are 100,000 Man United club members and 40,000 season ticket holders.

R IS FOR RELEGATION
It is hard to believe, but the club were relegated from the top-flight in 1975. But they bounced back at the first attempt as Second Division Champions.

S IS FOR STRETFORD END
Previously a huge behind-the-goal terrace at Old Trafford, but now an all-seater stand where United's most vocal fans sit.

T IS FOR TWELVE
The amount in millions that record signing Dwight Yorke cost United when they signed him from Aston Villa in August 1998.

U IS FOR UNBELIEVABLE
The manner in which United won the European Cup final in May. Two injury-time goals were enough to stage an incredible comeback against Bayern Munich.

V IS FOR VICTORY PARADE
The treble-winning United team of 1999 attracted a crowd of almost half-a-million when they paraded their trophies through the streets of Manchester last May.

W IS FOR WAYWARD BEHAVIOUR
Irish star George Best is perhaps the most gifted player to ever pull on the famous red shirt. He scored in United's European Cup final win over Benfica in 1968, and was made Footballer Of The Year and European Footballer Of The Year in the same year. Sadly his United career was cut short as he found it difficult to cope with the pressures of fame and he quit Old Trafford in 1972.

X IS FOR XTRA-TIME WINNER
Ryan Giggs' mazy run and strike against Arsenal last season was the last goal ever to be scored in an FA Cup semi-final replay. From this season tied semis will be decided on the night.

Y IS FOR YOUTH POLICY
When United lost their first league game of the 1995/96 season Alan Hansen famously said that they'd 'never win anything with kids'. However, United's young side, which included Phil and Gary Neville, Nicky Butt, Paul Scholes and David Beckham went on to do the double!

Z IS FOR ZERO
The number of times United have won the UEFA Cup – the only major trophy missing from the Old Trafford cabinet.

FAMOUS WINS
WIMBLEDON

TEAMS
WIMBLEDON v LIVERPOOL

MATCH
FA CUP FINAL

VENUE
WEMBLEY

DATE
MAY 15, 1988

STORY

Liverpool breezed into the FA Cup Final against Wimbledon as odds-on favourites. After all The Reds were already league champions, while the Londoners had been a Southern League club just 11 years before. The Dons proceeded to ruin 'Pool's party, however, with a typically battling display. The minnows took the lead on 36 minutes when Lawrie Sanchez headed a Dennis Wise free-kick past Bruce Grobbelaar. The real hero of the match was Dons 'keeper Dave Beasant, who saved a John Aldridge penalty half-an-hour before the end.

FINAL SCORE
DONS 1 LIVERPOOL 0

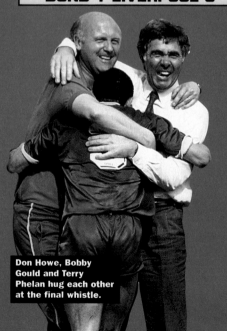

Don Howe, Bobby Gould and Terry Phelan hug each other at the final whistle.

Lawrie Sanchez heads Wimbledon's unlikely winner against the league champs.

Wimbledon's Dave Beasant holds aloft the FA Cup after becoming the first 'keeper to save a penalty in a Wembley cup final.

Vinnie Jones salutes Wimbledon's FA Cup Final heroics against Liverpool.

John Aldridge, who'd scored 11 penalties for Liverpool during the 1987/88 season, sees his spot-kick saved by Big Beas.

Shoot GREAT BOSSES

They win trophies and titles! They run about like loonies up and down the touchline! They're footie managers and they may not get paid as much as the flash stars they spend millions on but they're vital for a club's success. Here's SHOOT's guide to the best bosses of all time!

BRIAN CLOUGH – OL' BIG 'EAD

- **BORN** Middlesbrough. March 21, 1935
- **TEAMS MANAGED** Hartlepool United (1965-67); Derby County (1967-73); Brighton and Hove Albion (1973-74); Leeds United (1974); Nottingham Forest (1975-93)
- **HONOURS** English title (2); European Cup (2); League Cup (4); Cup Winners' Cup (2); European Super Cup (1)
- **THE LOWDOWN** At 29 Clough became the youngest man to ever pass the FA coaching badge, turning to management after his formidable career as a striker came to an end. After cutting his mangerial teeth at lowly Hartlepool, Clough went on an incredible pot hunting journey (15 trophies in 26 years) guiding Derby County to the League title in 1972. He did even better with equally untrendy east midlanders Nottingham Forest, taking them to the title in 1978 and following it up by winning back-to-back European Cups (1979, 1980). Despite winning numerous league and other assorted trophies, the one piece of silverware that eluded Ol' Big 'Ead was the FA Cup, reaching the semi-final in 1989 and the final in 1991.

🔵 **TOP BOSS RATING** ★★★★★

ALEX FERGUSON – BRITAIN'S BEST EVER BOSS

- **BORN** Govan, Scotland. December 31, 1941
- **TEAMS MANAGED** East Stirling (1974); St Mirren (1974-78); Aberdeen (1978-86); Scotland (1985-86); Man United (1986-present)
- **HONOURS** Aberdeen – Scottish title (3); Scottish Cup (4); Scottish League Cup (1); Cup Winners' Cup (1). United – English title (5); FA Cup (4); League Cup (1); European Cup (1); Cup Winners' Cup (1)
- **THE LOWDOWN** Officially the most successful ever manager in British football. The canny Scot made his name at Aberdeen, managing to break Celtic and Rangers' vice-like grip on domestic honours. His arrival in English football with United didn't produce immediate dividends, in fact rumour has it that Fergie was set to be sacked early in 1990. But his United team defeated Nottingham Forest in an FA Cup Fourth Round game and went on to win the trophy, saving his job in the process. Ferguson has not looked back since, with The Red Devils going on to dominate English, and now European, football in the '90s. Capable of signing big names and getting the best out of them, as well as developing his own top class youth stars.

🔵 **TOP BOSS RATING** ★★★★★

MATT BUSBY – UNITED'S FIRST GREAT MANAGER

- ■ **BORN** Orbiston. May 26, 1909 (Died: January 20, 1994)
- ■ **TEAMS MANAGED** Manchester United (1945-71)
- ■ **HONOURS** English title (5); FA Cup (2); European Cup (1)
- ■ **THE LOWDOWN** Until Alex Ferguson came along no United manager had been able to live under the massive shadow Matt Busby cast upon Old Trafford. In 1968 he became the first man to guide an English team to European Cup glory when his United side thumped Portuguese champions Benfica 4-1 at Wembley. The victory was particularly sweet as his side had, on three occasions, reached the semi-final only to lose. Sir Matt will also be remembered for his 'Busby Babes', the brilliant young United side he built in the 1950s which, having claimed three league titles, looked set to conquer Europe. Tragically his team was all but destroyed in the Munich air disaster of February, 1958, which left half the side dead or crippled, and Busby himself in a critical condition in hospital. He recovered and rebuilt his shattered side, making United great again. They finally fulfilled his European dream just a decade later.

⚽ TOP BOSS RATING ★★★★★

BOB PAISLEY – LIVERPOOL'S QUIET FOOTIE GENIUS

- ■ **BORN** County Durham. January 23, 1919 (Died: February 14, 1996)
- ■ **TEAMS MANAGED** Liverpool (1974-83)
- ■ **HONOURS** English title (6); European Cup (3); League Cup (3); UEFA Cup (1)
- ■ **THE LOWDOWN** Arguably English football's greatest ever manager, Paisley improved upon the acheivements of his predecessor Bill Shankly, winning 13 pieces of silverware in an extraordinary Anfield career. Having failed to win anything in his first season in charge of the famous Merseyside club, the quietly-spoken, unassuming Geordie led Liverpool to unparalleled success domestically and in Europe. In Paisley's nine years at the helm 'Pool finished outside the top flight's top two places only once (1980-81), claiming the title itself on six occasions. It is in Europe, however, that Paisley's record at Anfield is the most impressive. Under him Liverpool won three of their four European Cups, becoming the first British club to ever retain the trophy in 1978 following their victory over FC Bruges. Like Brian Clough, the only domestic trophy to elude Paisley was the FA Cup.

⚽ TOP BOSS RATING ★★★★★

BOBBY ROBSON – ENGLAND'S NEARLY MAN

- ■ **BORN** February 18, 1933
- ■ **TEAMS MANAGED** Vancouver Royals (1967-68); Fulham (1968); Ipswich (1969-82); England (1982-1990); PSV Eindhoven (1990-92); Sporting Lisbon (1992-93); Porto (1994-96); Barcelona (1996-98); PSV Eindhoven (1998)
- ■ **HONOURS** Ipswich – FA Cup (1); UEFA Cup (1). PSV Eindhoven – Dutch title (2). Porto – Portuguese Cup (1); Portuguese title (2). Barcelona – Spanish Cup (1); Cup Winners' Cup (1)
- ■ **THE LOWDOWN** Took Ipswich to glory in Europe and narrowly missed the league title with the same club twice. His career as England boss was a similar case of so near and yet so far. In 1986 the national side made the World Cup Quarter-Finals, going one better four years later, only to lose on penalties in the semis to West Germany. He quit England in 1990 for a long and varied career abroad, taking jobs in Spain, Portugal and Holland. Was controversially replaced as Barcelona boss in 1997 after leading them to a cup double, including the European Cup Winners' Cup. Was linked with a return to the England job before Kevin Keegan was given the nod instead.

⚽ TOP BOSS RATING ★★★

GEORGE GRAHAM – NORTH LONDON'S SILVERWARE KING

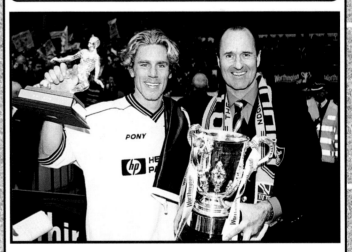

- ■ **BORN** Bargeddie, Scotland. November 30, 1944
- ■ **TEAMS MANAGED** Millwall (1982-86); Arsenal (1986-95); Leeds United (1996-98); Tottenham Hotspur (1998-present)
- ■ **HONOURS** Arsenal – English title (2); FA Cup (1); Cup Winners' Cup (1); League Cup (2). Tottenham – League Cup (1)
- ■ **THE LOWDOWN** Undoubtedly one of the most successful managers in the modern game, George built his twin league title captures at Arsenal on one of football's tightest defences. The Seaman/Lukic, Dixon, Adams, Bould/Keown, Winterburn defence that he assembled back in the late '80s/early '90s is, amazingly, still intact four seasons after he was forced out of Highbury over a bung scandal. Twelve months later Graham returned to the game at Leeds, turning a mediocre, relegation-threatened side into top five contenders. His controversial return to London, at Spurs, brought swift rewards with the capture of the Worthington (League) Cup after just six months in charge. It remains to be seen if the White Hart Lane side can now go on to emulate their Highbury rivals in the glory stakes.

⚽ TOP BOSS RATING ★★★

SIR ALF RAMSEY – WORLD CUP WINNING ENGLAND BOSS

BORN Dagenham. January 22, 1920 (Died April 28, 1999)
TEAMS MANAGED Ipswich Town (1955-63); England (1963-74); Birmingham City (1977-78)
HONOURS Ipswich – English title (1); England – World Cup (1)
THE LOWDOWN Ramsey made his name with Ipswich, gradually guiding Town from Third Division no hopers in 1955 to League champions in 1962 – the club's one and only title success. Ramsey departed Portman Road a year later to take up the England job vacated by Walter Winterbottom, famously claiming that England would win the World Cup in 1966 in their own back yard. Few believed him and that view point was given extra weight when his team kicked off the tournament with a disappointing goalless draw against Uruguay. In fact the South Americans were the first team to ever prevent England scoring at Wembley! After that hiccup, England didn't look back, defeating Mexico, France, Argentina and Portugal on their way to the Final against West Germany at Wembley. Ramsey's so-called 'Wingless Wonders' won the game 4-2 in extra-time and the victorious manager was rewarded with a knighthood in 1967.

TOP BOSS RATING *****

BILL SHANKLY – LIVERPOOL'S SAVIOUR

BORN Glenbuck, Scotland. September 2, 1913 (Died: September 29, 1981)
TEAMS MANAGED Carlisle United (1949-51); Grimsby Town (1951-54); Workington (1954-55); Huddersfield (1955-59); Liverpool (1959-74)
HONOURS English title (3); FA Cup (2); UEFA Cup (1)
THE LOWDOWN On paper Bill Shankly's achievements don't look much compared to those of his successor Bob Paisley, but, more than anyone, it was the tough-talking Scot who was responsible for Liverpool's rise to domestic and European prominence in the 1970s. When Shankly joined Liverpool they weren't even in the top-flight, although they'd narrowly missed promotion on a number of occasions. He took the club up as Champions of the old Division Two in 1962 and they won the title in 1964, following it up with an FA Cup victory the following season. Shankly's most important contribution to the Liverpool cause, however, was the formation of the famous Anfield Boot Room, an almost mystical place where the manager would pass on his footie philosophies and knowledge to his backroom staff and players. After Shankly's departure, the club was run by former Bootroom Boys, such as Bob Paisley and Joe Fagan, for years, with enormous success.

TOP BOSS RATING ****

TERRY VENABLES – ENGLAND'S CHEEKY CHAPPIE

■ **BORN** London. January 6, 1943
■ **TEAMS MANAGED** Crystal Palace (1976-80); QPR (1980-84); Barcelona (1984-87); Tottenham (1987-91); England (1994-96); Australia (1996-98); Crystal Palace (1998-99)
■ **HONOURS** Tottenham – FA Cup (1); Barcelona – Spanish title (1)
■ **THE LOWDOWN** 'El Tel' is most famous for two things. Firstly, he's the man responsible for taking England to the European Championship Semi-Finals in 1996 (their best performance in the tournament for 28 years). Secondly, he's the country's most controversial boss, falling out big-time with chairman Alan Sugar while at Spurs, and constantly portrayed in the media as a shady character who's only out for himself. Since his successful term in the England hot-seat Venables has seemingly been waiting for his next big challenge, biding his time with Crystal Palace, Portsmouth and the Australian national side until it comes along. Although Venners has only won two trophies as a boss, his popularity in England has never waned. He was the fans' choice to succeed Glenn Hoddle as boss of the national team and rarely a week goes by that he isn't linked with one major team or another.

TOP BOSS RATING ***

RUUD GULLIT – THE DUTCH MASTER

■ **BORN** Amsterdam, Holland. September 1, 1962
■ **TEAMS MANAGED** Chelsea (1996-98); Newcastle (1998-present)
■ **HONOURS** Chelsea – FA Cup (1)
■ **THE LOWDOWN** One of the most commanding and skilful players of all time, Gullit has also proved himself to be a dab hand at management. When Glenn Hoddle left Chelsea to manage England in 1996 the Dutchman stepped up to become the club's player/manager. After lifting the FA Cup in his first season in charge at Stamford Bridge (The Blues' first major piece of silverware in 26 years) it seemed that the only way was up for the dreadlocked star and his team of fancy foreign signings. But a clash of egos with chairman Ken Bates over a new contract saw the Dutchman sensationally sacked. Ironically, Chelsea were second in the League, in the Quarter-Finals of the Cup Winners' Cup and the Semi-Finals of the League Cup at the time of his dismissal! After that Gullit retreated to Amsterdam to lick his wounds, but it wasn't long before he was snapped up by Newcastle, who had just sacked Kenny Dalglish. In his first season Gullit returned to Wembley for an FA Cup Final. This time, however, his team lost – 2-0 to Man United.

TOP BOSS RATING **

DON REVIE – LEEDS & ENGLAND HERO OR VILLAIN

- **BORN** Middlesbrough July 10, 1927 (Died: May 26, 1989)
- **TEAMS MANAGED** Leeds United (1961-74); England (1974-77); United Arab Emirates (1977-80)
- **HONOURS** Leeds – English title (2); FA Cup (1); League Cup (1); Fairs Cup (UEFA Cup) (2)
- **THE LOWDOWN** Like Bill Shankly at Liverpool, when Revie took control at Leeds they were Division Two strugglers. In fact the Elland Roaders only just escaped relegation in his first season in charge. However, it wasn't long before they won promotion, finishing second in their first two seasons in the top-flight. United won Revie his first title in 1969 and although they never quite managed to dominate the game in the same way that Liverpool and Man United eventually did, Leeds still notched up six trophies during his managerial reign. The Leeds silverware collection included winning the Fairs Cup twice, once over two-legs against Italian giants Juventus. Revie left for the England job in 1974 but failed in his bid to guide them to the 1978 World Cup. Breaking his contract, he controversially quit the national side to sample the riches of the United Arab Emirates in the Middle East.

⚽ TOP BOSS RATING ★★★

JOHN 'JOCK' STEIN – THE BHOYS' TOP BOY

- **BORN** Burnbank, Scotland. October 5, 1925 (Died: November 10, 1985)
- **TEAMS MANAGED** Dunfermline (1960); Hibernian (1964-65); Celtic (1965-78); Leeds (1978); Scotland (1978-85)
- **HONOURS** Celtic – European Cup (1); Scottish title (10); Scottish Cup (9); Scottish League Cup (6)
- **THE LOWDOWN** In 1967 Stein (pictured above with a young Alex Ferguson) became the first British boss to lift the European Cup. His Celtic side defeated Italian giants Inter Milan 2-1 in Lisbon, Portugal (hence their 'Lisbon Lions' nickname). Stein was equally successful domestically, presiding over The Bhoys' lengthiest reign at the top of Scottish football. They won nine titles in a row between 1966 and 1974, a record that stood until 1997 when it was finally matched by Rangers. Stein tried his hand at management in England but his stay at Leeds lasted just 44 days! He next became manager of the Scottish national side, guiding them to World Cup qualification in 1982. He tragically died at Cardiff's Ninian Park in the players' tunnel during a match with Wales – just months before the 1986 World Cup Finals in Mexico.

⚽ TOP BOSS RATING ★★★★★

FRANZ BECKENBAUER – THE COOL KAISER

- **BORN** Munich, Germany. September 11, 1945
- **TEAMS MANAGED** West Germany (1984-90); Marseille (1990-91); Bayern Munich (1993-94 and 1996)
- **HONOURS** West Germany – World Cup (1); Bayern Munich – UEFA Cup (1), German title (1)
- **THE LOWDOWN** One of Germany's greatest and most respected players, Beckenbauer successfully translated his skills on the pitch to management, first as the boss of the West German national team and later as coach of his beloved Bayern Munich. His West German side broke English hearts on their way to victory in the 1990 World Cup in Italy, beating Bobby Robson's men in a Semi-Final penalty shoot-out and making Gazza cry! The Germans went on to win the tournament in a disappointing Final with Argentina and Beckenbauer left a happy man. He returned to top grade management with French side Marseille, where he had a short and rather unhappy spell, but rediscovered his midas touch at Bayern, where he won the German title in 1994. He became the club's president soon after, returning briefly to the manager's hot seat to lead Bayern to UEFA Cup glory in 1996.

⚽ TOP BOSS RATING ★★★★

ARSENE WENGER – ARSENAL'S FOOTIE PROFESSOR

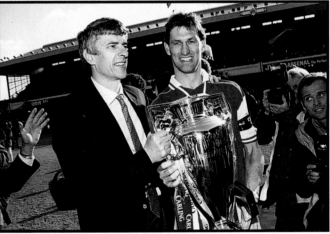

- **BORN** Strasbourg, France. October 22, 1948
- **TEAMS MANAGED** Nancy (1984-87); Monaco (1987-94); Grampus Eight (Japan) (1995-96); Arsenal (1996-present)
- **HONOURS** Monaco – French Championship (1); French Cup (1). Arsenal – English title (1); FA Cup (1)
- **THE LOWDOWN** The appropriately named Arsene became Arsenal manager in 1996, having carved out a reputation in France and Japan as one of football's most astute and progressive coaches. It didn't take long for the Frenchman to make his name in England, in May 1998 becoming the first foreign manager to win the league title. His reputation as a Highbury legend was cemented when he and his team claimed the FA Cup, and with it the Double, just a few weeks later. Last season he proved that his success was no flash in the pan as Arsenal pushed Man United all the way for the league title in one of the tightest contests in Premiership history. Although the press have been keen to link the Frenchman with a move away from Highbury it seems certain Wenger will stay for the forseeable future, as his plans to make Arsenal a real force in Europe start to take shape.

⚽ TOP BOSS RATING ★★★

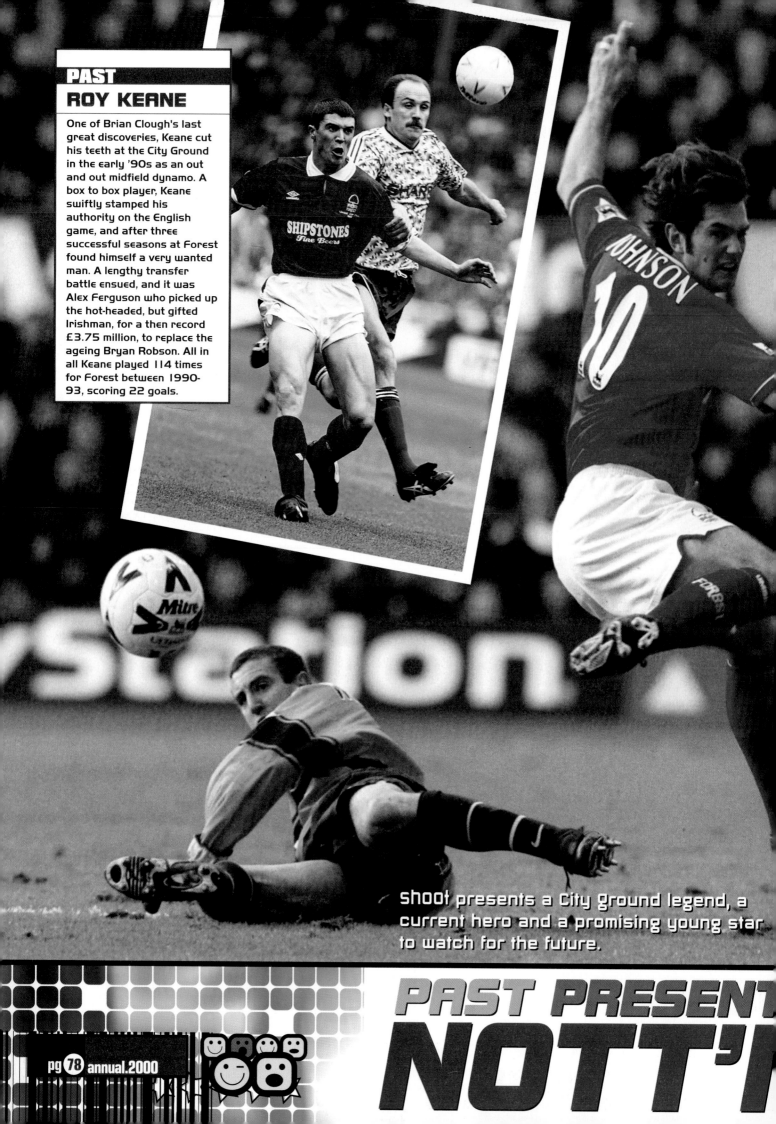

PAST
ROY KEANE

One of Brian Clough's last great discoveries, Keane cut his teeth at the City Ground in the early '90s as an out and out midfield dynamo. A box to box player, Keane swiftly stamped his authority on the English game, and after three successful seasons at Forest found himself a very wanted man. A lengthy transfer battle ensued, and it was Alex Ferguson who picked up the hot-headed, but gifted Irishman, for a then record £3.75 million, to replace the ageing Bryan Robson. All in all Keane played 114 times for Forest between 1990-93, scoring 22 goals.

Shoot presents a City Ground legend, a current hero and a promising young star to watch for the future.

PAST PRESENT
NOTT'I

MARLON HAREWOOD

The 20-year-old defender made his debut in a Division One game against West Brom in May 1998 and has been battling for a regular first team place ever since. The London born stopper also has an eye for goal, and scored in two Worthington Cup matches last term, along with a fine strike against Middlesbrough. With Forest short on cash and desperate to rebuild expect Harewood, who has enjoyed loan spells with Ipswich and Finnish side FC Haka, to finally claim his place in the sun.

PRESENT

ANDY JOHNSON

Andy's growing stature as a combative midfielder could be enhanced this term as Forest seek to bounce back from yet another Premiership relegation. The powerful Welshman was bought from Norwich in 1997, where he had spent six seasons, becoming a first team regular in his last two. At the City Ground Johnson has continued to build on the reputation he gained at his former club as a cultured performer with a steely side to his game.

UTURE FOREST

A TO Z

SHEFFIELD WEDNESDAY
FOOTBALL CLUB PLC
Consilio et Animis
Est. 1867

A IS FOR ARSENAL
In 1993, for the first time ever, both the FA Cup Final and League Cup Final were contested by the same clubs – Wednesday and Arsenal. Sadly, The Owls lost both games!

B IS FOR BIG RON
Ron Atkinson was boss at Hillsborough between 1989 and 1991, and brought silverware to the club for the first time in 56 years after The Owls beat Man United in the League Cup Final in 1991. He returned to the club as caretaker manager in 1997.

C IS FOR CRICKET CLUB
Wednesday were founded by members of a cricket club in 1867. The cricket club was called Wednesday because the team met to play on that afternoon of each week.

D IS FOR DISMISSAL
Italian Paolo Di Canio's career at Sheffield Wednesday ended in disgrace a year ago when he was sent off against Arsenal. In an extraordinary sequence of events, he pushed referee Paul Alcock over and received a 12-match ban for his bad behaviour.

E IS FOR ENGLAND STAR
Chris Waddle joined The Owls in 1992 after a successful spell at Marseille. His mazy, dribbling skills helped his side to the League and FA Cup finals of 1993. In the same year he was named the Football Writers' Player Of The Year.

F IS FOR FOLK HERO
Derek Dooley was a sensation upfront for the club in the early 1950s, scoring a club record 46 goals in 1952. But tragedy struck in 1953 when he suffered a broken leg which became infected with gangrene and had to be amputated. He became club manager in 1971, but was sacked a year later.

G IS FOR GOALS, GOALS, GOALS
Wednesday's biggest win was against Halliwell in the First Round of the FA Cup back in 1891. Their worst defeat occurred against Aston Villa (10-0) in 1912.

H IS FOR HARKES
John Harkes became the first American to ever score at Wembley when he netted for The Owls in the League Cup Final in 1993 after just nine minutes.

I IS FOR INTERNATIONAL STARS
There have been some fine foreign players to sign for Wednesday, with Swedish full-back Roland Nilsson perhaps the most loved and successful at the club. Nilsson joined in 1989 and played 181 flawless games in five years before leaving in 1994.

J IS FOR JUDGE
In 1983, Owls fan Bob Montgomery took the club to court under the Trades Descriptions Act after they lost an FA Cup replay. He argued that the football played by the side had been so bad that his entrance fee had been taken under false pretences, but the judge disagreed and found against him.

K IS FOR Tony KAY
Notorious for being involved in the biggest scandal in British football. He served time in prison for receiving bribes whilst playing for Wednesday in the early '60s and was arrested after his transfer to Everton.

L IS FOR LOWER LEAGUES
Wednesday have been relegated no less than nine times in their history.

M IS FOR MANAGER

Danny Wilson took over as The Owls' boss in the summer of 1998, and is regarded as one of the game's best young managers, having taken Barnsley into the Premiership for the first time in the club's history in 1997.

N IS FOR NICKNAMES

Sheffield Wednesday are known affectionately as The Owls. The name originates from the Sheffield district of Owlerton, which is where the Hillsborough ground is situated.

O IS FOR OLD

Formed in 1867, Sheffield Wednesday are one of the oldest football clubs in the world and have always had blue and white as their club colours.

P IS FOR PHYSIOTHERAPY

A subject ex-striker David Hirst knows all about. Having joined the club in 1985, he left for Southampton in 1998 having managed only 294 games in almost 13 injury hit years. However, his goal tally of 106 still makes him one of the most successful Owls strikers ever.

Q IS FOR QUICKEST GOAL

Charlie Tomlinson holds the record for the fastest goal scored by an Owls player, netting after 12 seconds against Preston in 1949.

R IS FOR RECORD BREAKING PLAYER

Andy Wilson holds a double Owls record, having played the most games for the club (545) and scored the most goals (216).

S IS FOR SO YOUNG

'Keeper Peter Fox was just 15 years and 269 days old when he made his senior Owls debut on March 31, 1973.

T IS FOR TRAGEDY

Hillsborough became the scene of Britain's worst football disaster during an FA Cup Semi-Final game between Liverpool and Nottingham Forest in 1989. 96 people died in a crush resulting from overcrowding at the Leppings Lane end.

U IS FOR UNBEATEN RUN

The longest Wednesday have managed to go without losing is 19 matches, between December 1960 and April 1961.

V IS FOR VICTORIOUS

Wednesday's haul of silverware won over the years reads: four League titles (the last in 1930), three FA Cups and a League Cup.

W IS FOR WORST START

It took 11 League games in the 1977-78 season for Wednesday to record a win. Five draws and five losses had been the best they could manage up until that point.

X IS FOR XMAS TIME

The Christmas of 1911 was full of great tidings of joy for Wednesday. In their Boxing Day clash against Sunderland, they found themselves 7-0 up at half-time. They eventually ran out 8-0 winners.

Y IS FOR YOUTH DEVELOPMENT

The man who is responsible for the development of young English players, Howard Wilkinson, was once a player and manager at Wednesday. As a winger, he scored 19 goals in 129 games. As a manager, he took over in 1983 and won promotion to the First Division in his first season, taking the team to fifth place in the top-flight in 1986.

Z IS FOR ZENITH

The high-point, or zenith, of the club's success came in the early 1900s. Wednesday won back-to-back titles in 1903 and 1904, and came close to winning a league and cup double in the latter season. Unfortunately, they were defeated in that year's FA Cup Semi-Final.

FAMOUS WINS
RANGERS

TEAMS
RANGERS v LEEDS

MATCH
EUROPEAN CUP SECOND RD

VENUE
IBROX STADIUM

DATE
OCTOBER 21, 1992

STORY

A two-legged European Cup tie billed The Battle Of Britain saw Rangers progress to the Champions League stage of the competition. English champs Leeds started the first-leg at Ibrox perfectly, going ahead with a goal from Scotsman Gary McAllister in the first minute. It was a lead that a John Lukic own goal cancelled out 20 minutes later, with Ally McCoist putting 'Gers ahead eight minutes before half-time. Even the presence of Eric Cantona couldn't lift the Yorkshire side in the second half, meaning the Glasgow giants carried their slender advantage to Elland Road, where they also won 2-1 in the second-leg.

FINAL SCORE
RANGERS 2 LEEDS 1

Ian Ferguson gets the better of Tony Dorigo as the Battle Of Britain heats up at Ibrox.

Gary McAllistair celebrates his first minute goal – a 30-yard curled free-kick into the top corner of the Rangers' net.

John Lukic pushes David McPherson's header away only to see Ally McCoist bury the loose ball in the back of the net. The goal won the tie for Rangers.

Even the magical skills of Eric Cantona couldn't lift Leeds to European Cup glory.

Leeds 'keeper John Lukic looks back in horror as the ball rebounds off his fist and into the United net.

Shoot SUPER

Everyone has their own opinions on who the world's best striker is. Is it Michael Owen? Ronaldo? Gabriel Batistuta? In hope of ending the debate forever (some chance!) here's the SHOOT lowdown on the world's best hitmen.

ALAN SHEARER

- **TEAM** Newcastle & England
- **PREVIOUS TEAMS** Southampton, Blackburn
- **AGE 29**
- **CREDENTIALS** England's captain might not be the player he was a couple of years ago but he still has one of the best goalscoring records in the world. The first player to score 100 Premiership goals, he set a new British transfer record when he signed for Newcastle for £15 million in 1996.
- **STRENGTHS** As tough as they come, hard to shake off the ball and possesses one of the fastest shots in the game. Also great in the air.
- **WEAKNESSES** Since coming back from a serious ankle injury last year, his critics claim he's not as quick or as strong as he was, and the number of goals he scored last season was low compared to previous years.

SHOOTING	95
HEADING	95
PASSING	70
DRIBBLING	70
WORKRATE	90
SHOOT RATING	**84**

MICHAEL OWEN

- **TEAM** Liverpool & England
- **PREVIOUS TEAMS** none
- **AGE 19**
- **CREDENTIALS** A year after bursting on to the Premiership scene, the teenager scored one of the most talked-about goals of France '98 for England v Argentina. Slammed in two hat-tricks early on in the '98/99 season and finished as joint top Premiership scorer.
- **STRENGTHS** Blistering pace and huge confidence. Has shown amazing maturity beyond his years and has terrorised every defender he's come up against – including some of the world's best-known names.
- **WEAKNESSES** As one of the game's smaller strikers, he's not much of a target man, and isn't going to score with too many headers.

SHOOTING	90
HEADING	60
PASSING	75
DRIBBLING	90
WORKRATE	80
SHOOT RATING	**79**

STRIKERS!

DWIGHT YORKE

- **TEAM** Manchester United & Trinidad and Tobago
- **PREVIOUS TEAMS** Aston Villa
- **AGE 27**
- **CREDENTIALS** Known as the smiling face of football, the man from Tobago had a brilliant first season at Man United after his transfer from Aston Villa, and as well as picking up three medals at the end of it, finished joint top Premiership scorer.
- **STRENGTHS** Has shown remarkable consistency throughout his career and rarely suffers a goal drought. Great footwork and a demon inside the area, defenders certainly can't relax when he's around.
- **WEAKNESSES** Dwight's height means he lacks a little bit of presence and is never going to be a major threat in the air.

SHOOTING	90
HEADING	65
PASSING	70
DRIBBLING	80
WORKRATE	80
SHOOT RATING	**77**

ANDY COLE

- **TEAM** Manchester United & England
- **PREVIOUS TEAMS** Arsenal, Bristol City, Newcastle
- **AGE 27**
- **CREDENTIALS** Rejected by Arsenal, Andy went to Newcastle after a spell at Bristol City and really found his goalscoring boots at St James' Park, helping the Geordies back into the Premiership. His move to Man United came as a shock, but ultimately has proved to be a success.
- **STRENGTHS** A great team player, he is able to hold the ball up, run at defenders and find space in the box.
- **WEAKNESSES** Often needs several chances to score and is sometimes accused of missing the easy efforts, showing a lack of composure at the vital moment.

SHOOTING	80
HEADING	70
PASSING	70
DRIBBLING	70
WORKRATE	90
SHOOT RATING	**76**

ROBBIE FOWLER

- **TEAM** Liverpool & England
- **PREVIOUS TEAMS** none
- **AGE** 24
- **CREDENTIALS** A real goal machine who broke into the Liverpool team in the early '90s and has been there ever since, even successfully overcoming a long-term leg injury that kept him out for eight months and forced him to miss France '98. Set to become an England regular if he can transfer his club form on to the international stage.
- **STRENGTHS** Deadly in the penalty area, able to shoot with both feet and not bad in the air either. Great pace, too.
- **WEAKNESSES** Suspect temperament and has been in trouble for provoking other players and stirring up the crowd.

SHOOTING	95
HEADING	85
PASSING	70
DRIBBLING	80
WORKRATE	75

SHOOT RATING 81

DENNIS BERGKAMP

- **TEAM** Arsenal & Holland
- **PREVIOUS TEAMS** Ajax, Inter Milan
- **AGE** 30
- **CREDENTIALS** Has established himself as one of the world's top forwards after success with Arsenal and goals for Holland. The inspiration behind Arsenal's double of last year, he struggled to find his form in the first half of last season, but came back strongly in the New Year.
- **STRENGTHS** One of the best footballing brains in the Prem, Bergkamp knows a good run when he sees it and has the ability to play the right pass. An excellent finisher himself, a boss's dream when he's on top of his game.
- **WEAKNESSES** His play is very dependent on his mood. Sometimes he appears unfocussed and uninterested. Can't fly to away games in Europe.

SHOOTING	95
HEADING	70
PASSING	100
DRIBBLING	80
WORKRATE	75

SHOOT RATING 84

GIANFRANCO ZOLA

- **TEAM** Chelsea & Italy
- **PREVIOUS TEAMS** Nuorese, Torres, Napoli, Parma
- **AGE** 34
- **CREDENTIALS** Probably the most successful of the recent Italian imports into the Premiership, the diminutive striker won the Player Of The Year award in 1997 and helped Chelsea to their best ever trophy-winning spell.
- **STRENGTHS** A tremendous understanding of the game, instinctively able to play team-mates into dangerous positions, able to strike from distance and turn defenders inside out with his clever footwork.
- **WEAKNESSES** At the age of 34, he is certainly past his best and can struggle with the pace of the Premiership, fading out of games and being increasingly substituted.

SHOOTING	85
HEADING	60
PASSING	90
DRIBBLING	95
WORKRATE	90

SHOOT RATING 84

DARREN HUCKERBY

- **TEAM** Coventry City
- **PREVIOUS TEAMS** Lincoln, Newcastle
- **AGE** 23
- **CREDENTIALS** Two successive seasons of regular goalscoring at Highfield Road have placed Huckerby near the top of the list of the best up-and-coming strikers in the Premiership. Regularly linked to big money moves to Old Trafford and Anfield.
- **STRENGTHS** Incredible pace and excellent footwork make Huckerby one of the hardest players to stop when he's in a one-on-one situation.
- **WEAKNESSES** Sometimes lacks composure in front of goal and occasionally prone to holding onto the ball for too long. Has also suffered a few very long goal droughts.

SHOOTING	80
HEADING	70
PASSING	70
DRIBBLING	85
WORKRATE	80

RATING 77

DION DUBLIN

- ■ **TEAM** Aston Villa & England
- ■ **PREVIOUS TEAMS** Cambridge United, Manchester United, Coventry
- ■ **AGE** 30
- ■ **CREDENTIALS** Able to play either in the centre of defence or as a striker, Dublin is the kind of player every manager would want in his squad. A man with a big heart and the stomach for a battle.
- ■ **STRENGTHS** His greatest asset is his physical strength. A terrific athlete and very mobile, Dublin is equally effective meeting a cross with his head or letting rip with a shot from outside the box.
- ■ **WEAKNESSES** Dion has never been renowned for his pace and that could be one of the reasons behind his failure to break into the England squad on a regular basis.

SHOOTING	75
HEADING	90
PASSING	70
DRIBBLING	70
WORKRATE	90

SHOOT RATING   **79**

JIMMY FLOYD HASSELBAINK

- ■ **TEAM** Leeds United & Holland
- ■ **PREVIOUS TEAMS** Campomairorense, Boavista
- ■ **AGE** 27
- ■ **CREDENTIALS** One of the reasons behind the resurgence of Leeds, Jimmy took no time at all in becoming the No.1 striker at Elland Road. Finished joint top Premiership scorer at the end of last season and his late strike against Arsenal in May cemented Leeds' place in Europe.
- ■ **STRENGTHS** Possesses good pace and can tap them in from six yards or lash them in from further out.
- ■ **WEAKNESSES** Prone to off days when he can't seem to stay onside, or seems to go AWOL on the pitch and lacks understanding with some of the players around him.

SHOOTING	80
HEADING	85
PASSING	75
DRIBBLING	75
WORKRATE	70

RATING   **77**

EMILE HESKEY

- ■ **TEAM** Leicester City
- ■ **PREVIOUS TEAMS** none
- ■ **AGE** 21
- ■ **CREDENTIALS** With a few seasons' experience already under his belt, Heskey has already caught the attention of England manager Kevin Keegan and is all set for a fruitful career.
- ■ **STRENGTHS** His physique is not unlike that of a champion boxer, and his strength makes it almost impossible for a defender to shake him off the ball, giving him a decided advantage in the air and at set pieces.
- ■ **WEAKNESSES** Not renowned for his pace and has been a little injury-prone in the past year or so. He is also falling behind other up-and-coming players like Michael Owen and Alan Smith in the goalscoring charts.

SHOOTING	80
HEADING	90
PASSING	70
DRIBBLING	75
WORKRATE	80

RATING   **79**

TORE ANDRE FLO

- ■ **TEAM** Chelsea & Norway
- ■ **PREVIOUS TEAMS** Sogndal, Tromso, Brann
- ■ **AGE** 26
- ■ **CREDENTIALS** One of the tallest players in the Premiership, Flo arrived at Chelsea to play understudy to the likes of Zola, Mark Hughes and Casiraghi, earning a reputation as a goalscoring supersub. When Hughes left and Casiraghi got injured, he got his chance to play a regular role in The Blues' Premiership push.
- ■ **STRENGTHS** Excellent balance, despite his height, good ball control and, not surprisingly, a tough customer in the air.
- ■ **WEAKNESSES** Misses too many easy chances and, despite a prolonged run in the Chelsea line-up, has been unable to show consistency.

SHOOTING	80
HEADING	90
PASSING	80
DRIBBLING	70
WORKRATE	80

RATING: **80**

KANU

- **TEAM** Arsenal & Nigeria
- **PREVIOUS TEAMS** Inter Milan
- **AGE 22**
- **CREDENTIALS** Burst onto the scene when Arsene Wenger signed him from Inter Milan in early 1999. Immediately started scoring with regular ease, mainly as a substitute, to help put Arsenal's waning Championship hopes right back on course.
- **STRENGTHS** Amazing ability on the ball. Good first touch, top dribbling skills and classy finisher – a real crowd-pleaser.
- **WEAKNESSES** Despite his goals, he was unable to establish himself in The Gunners' first 11. Expect that problem to disappear once he gets properly used to the pace of the English game.

SHOOTING	90
HEADING	70
PASSING	80
DRIBBLING	80
WORKRATE	70
RATING	**78**

ALAN SMITH

- **TEAM** Leeds United
- **PREVIOUS TEAMS** none
- **AGE 18**
- **CREDENTIALS** One of a crop of talented players to graduate from a very successful Leeds youth team, he has become a first-team regular at an extremely young age.
- **STRENGTHS** A real goal-poacher who does his deadly work in and around the six-yard box. Very confident and undaunted by the pace and strength of the Premiership.
- **WEAKNESSES** A dozen yellow cards in his first full season suggest Alan needs to curb his temper and learn not to retaliate against the defenders who foul him or try and put him off his game.

SHOOTING	85
HEADING	65
PASSING	70
DRIBBLING	70
WORKRATE	85
RATING	**75**

RONALDO

- **TEAM** Inter Milan & Brazil
- **PREVIOUS TEAMS** Social Ramos Club, Sao Cristovao, Cruzeiro Belo PSV Eindhoven, Barcelona
- **AGE 22**
- **CREDENTIALS** Probably the most famous player in the world, he won the European Player Of The Year award when barely out of his teens. Bubble burst somewhat in the World Cup Final when a combination of stress and injury made him the scapegoat for his team's 3-0 defeat against France.
- **STRENGTHS** Unbelievable pace and close control, confident finisher with either foot and a player who lives to score goals.
- **WEAKNESSES** Years of playing too many games when not fully fit have taken their toll and Ronaldo has become injury prone.

SHOOTING	95
HEADING	75
PASSING	80
DRIBBLING	80
WORKRATE	85
RATING	**83**

ANDREI SHEVCHENKO

- **TEAM** AC Milan & Russia
- **PREVIOUS TEAMS** Dinamo Kiev
- **AGE 22**
- **CREDENTIALS** One of the most prolific strikers to come out of Eastern Europe in recent years, the Ukrainian has been rewarded for his success with a dream move to Italian champions AC Milan after several seasons at Dinamo Kiev.
- **STRENGTHS** Has already been dubbed 'the Cyclone from the East' by the Italian press and is certainly very quick with an ability to find space.
- **WEAKNESSES** Can fade out of games and occasionally lacks composure in front of goal. He faces a big season as players from the Russian republics have often flattered to deceive after big-money moves to the west.

SHOOTING	95
HEADING	70
PASSING	70
DRIBBLING	85
WORKRATE	75
RATING	**79**

HENRIK LARSSON

- **TEAM** Celtic & Sweden
- **PREVIOUS TEAMS** Feyenoord
- **AGE** 27
- **CREDENTIALS** The dreadlocked Swede is a real favourite at Celtic Park and won the Scottish Player Of The Year award for 1999 after netting another hatful of goals.
- **STRENGTHS** Quick-footed and quick-witted, Larsson is prepared to try the unlikely and the outrageous as well as putting away the more easy, less spectacular chances.
- **WEAKNESSES** His light frame means he can be out-muscled by defenders – if they are quick enough to catch him. He can also be over-indulgent on the ball at times, running himself into trouble.

SHOOTING	85
HEADING	65
PASSING	70
DRIBBLING	85
WORKRATE	80

RATING 77

GABRIEL BATISTUTA

- **TEAM** Fiorentina & Argentina
- **PREVIOUS TEAMS** Newell's O.B., River Plate, Boca Juniors
- **AGE** 30
- **CREDENTIALS** After eight years at Italian side Fiorentina, 'Batigol' has become the highest-scoring player ever in Serie A and scored in a record 11 games in a row in 1994. A regular in the Argentinian side, he has turned down lucrative moves to Parma and Manchester United to stay in Florence.
- **STRENGTHS** A real team player, Batistuta is able to score goals any which way he likes; free-kicks, headers, through balls, tap-ins and long-range efforts are all within his capabilities.
- **WEAKNESSES** Batistuta insists he is not a complete striker, and is still looking to improve his left-foot shot.

SHOOTING	90
HEADING	80
PASSING	80
DRIBBLING	80
WORKRATE	90

RATING 84

CHRISTIAN VIERI

- **TEAM** Inter Milan & Italy
- **PREVIOUS TEAMS** Prato, Torino, Pisa, Ravena, Venesia, Atalanta, Juventus, Atletico Madrid, Lazio
- **AGE** 26
- **CREDENTIALS** Made a name for himself at France '98 by scoring the bulk of Italy's goals. Became the world's most expensive player when Inter paid fellow Serie A side Lazio £28 million for his signature.
- **STRENGTHS** Has the build of a typical English centre-forward which makes him deadly in the air and excellent at holding up the ball.
- **WEAKNESSES** Tends to be argumentative and moody when things don't go his way. Lacks a bit of pace and his height means that the teams he plays in can resort to playing too much hit-and-hope football.

SHOOTING	85
HEADING	95
PASSING	70
DRIBBLING	70
WORKRATE	85

RATING 81

OLIVER BIERHOFF

- **TEAM** AC Milan & Germany
- **PREVIOUS TEAMS** Bayer Urdingen, Hamburg, B. Moenchengladbach, Casino Salzburg, Ascoli, Udinese
- **AGE** 31
- **CREDENTIALS** One of Germany's few remaining truly world-class performers, the AC Milan striker came late onto the international scene, making his debut at the age of 27 and really establishing himself by scoring the Golden Goal winner in the 1996 European Championship Final.
- **STRENGTHS** A well-built athlete, he is a real danger in the air and is a master goal-poacher in the six-yard box.
- **WEAKNESSES** Not likely to ever win a sprint race, Bierhoff's game has never been about pace.

SHOOTING	85
HEADING	90
PASSING	75
DRIBBLING	70
WORKRATE	85

RATING 81

a legend from the Portman road past, a hero from its present and a young star to watch for the future.

PAST

TERRY BUTCHER

During the Ipswich glory years under Bobby Robson, Town could boast a bevy of internationals in their line-up. Butcher was a prime example and was arguably the finest English defender of the '80s. When Robson got the nod for the England job Butcher was always an automatic choice, winning his 77th and final cap at Italia '90, where England made the World Cup Semi-Finals.

PAST PRESENT IPSWIC

PRESENT
RICHARD WRIGHT

The natural long term successor to David Seaman, Wright broke into the full England squad last season after years as the first choice under-21 'keeper. Wright looks set for a big future between the sticks after consistently thwarting Division One defences over the past three seasons. Last term he helped take Town to the very brink of promotion to the Premiership, only to be denied by Bradford's win at Wolves. Town will be pooling their limited resouces to try and hang onto their hottest property.

FUTURE
TITUS BRAMBLE

Stylish Suffolk-born 17-year-old central defender, who was handed his first team debut last seaon by boss George Burley against Sheffield United. The Blues' boss has since given the youngster a handful of games, and he looks set for a regular place in the coming seasons. Bramble, despite his tender years, has been with Ipswich since he was snapped up by the Suffolk club at the age of eight. His ambition is to one day be as good a player as his hero, Sol Campbell.

A TO Z

A IS FOR APPEARANCES
The player who has made the most league appearances for the club is Alec McNair. He played 583 times for Celtic in the early 1900s, before retiring at the age of 41.

B IS FOR The BHOYS
Celtic's nickname. The Glasgow team have also been occasionally known as The 'Tic, The Hoops and The Celts.

C IS FOR CLEAN SWEEP
Celtic have won the Scottish treble of league title, League Cup and FA Cup on two occasions – in 1966/67 and 1968/69.

D IS FOR Kenny DALGLISH
One of Celtic's all time greatest players. He joined the club as a youngster in 1967, helping them to four league titles before he was sold to Liverpool for £440,000 in 1977. Now back at Celtic as Director Of Football Operations.

E IS FOR EMBARRASSING
Celtic were thumped 8-0 by Motherwell in a league match back in April, 1937. Unsurprisingly it's their biggest ever defeat.

F IS FOR FEYENOORD
The team that prevented Celtic from becoming the first British team to win the European Cup twice. The Dutch side defeated The Bhoys 2-1 in the 1970 final after extra time.

G IS FOR GOALSCORING
James McGrory holds two club goalscoring records. He hit 50 goals in one season in 1935/36, and between 1922 and 1939 scored 397 times for The Bhoys.

H IS FOR HENRIK LARSSON
Celtic's flash Swedish forward with the distinctive dreadlocks. He was signed from Dutch side Feyenoord in 1997 for under half-a-million pounds and hit 38 goals in 48 appearances last season.

I IS FOR INDIA
The birthplace of striker Abdul Salim, who played in the reserves for Celtic back in the 1930s. Legend has it that he wore bandages on his feet instead of boots – ouch!

J IS FOR Mo JOHNSTON
The club's most controversial player of all time. he played for The Bhoys in the mid-'80s before joining French side Nantes. He returned to Scottish football in 1989 with hated rivals Rangers, a move that didn't go down too well with Celtic fans to say the very least!

K IS FOR KILMARNOCK
The team that ended an amazing Celtic league winning streak on April 21, 1917. The undefeated run had started on November 13, 1915 and went on to last 62 matches.

L IS FOR LISBON LIONS
The nickname of the Celtic team which became the first British side to win the European Cup in 1967. They beat Italian side Inter Milan 2-1 in Lisbon (hence the name) to lift the trophy.

M IS FOR Billy McNEIL
Probably Celtic's most famous player. Nicknamed Caesar, the defender captained The Bhoys to European Cup glory in 1967 and holds the club's all-time appearance record – 787 matches in all competitions between 1958 and 1975. He also successfully managed the club to four league titles in the late '70s/early '80s.

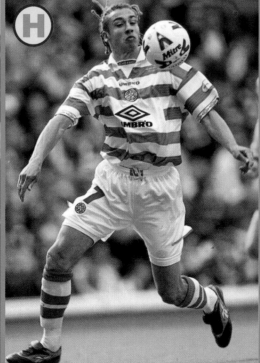

CELTIC
★★★★★

A HISTORY OF THE GLASGOW GIANTS ALL THE WAY FROM A TO Z.

N IS FOR NUMBER ONE
Goalkeeper Pat Bonner is one of Celtic's most celebrated stars. He joined The Bhoys in 1978 and went on to become the club's most capped player, appearing 80 times for the Republic Of Ireland. His penalty-saving heroics at the World Cup in 1990 saw his country make it to the Quarter-Finals.

O IS FOR OLD FIRM
The name given to Rangers and Celtic, the two giants of Scottish football. The rivalry between them, mostly based on religious differences, is arguably the most intense in the world.

P IS FOR PARADISE
The nickname given to The Bhoys' recently refurbished home ground, Celtic Park. With a capacity of over 60,000 it's currently Britain's biggest club stadium.

Q IS FOR QUITE A FEW
92,000 supporters turned up at Celtic Park to see The Bhoys take on arch rivals Rangers on January 1, 1938 – it's a club record.

R IS FOR RELEGATION
There's no such thing for Celtic, having never been out of the top division since the Scottish League was formed in 1890. Although they did finish 12th once!

S IS FOR Jock STEIN
Celtic's greatest ever manager. It was he that presided over The Bhoys' two most amazing achievements – winning the European Cup in 1967 and claiming nine league titles in a row between 1966 and 1974. He went on to become manager of Leeds and eventually Scotland.

T IS FOR TRY SPELLING THAT!
Polish forward Dariusz Dziekanowski joined Celtic in 1989. He once scored four goals in a European tie with Partizan Belgrade and his last name is pronounced Jack-an-ovski. He left Celtic Park in 1992.

U IS FOR UNBEARABLE
On May 2, 1999 Rangers beat Celtic 3-0 in one of the most ill-tempered Old Firm derbies ever. The result was particularly upsetting for Bhoys' fans as it meant that their arch rivals had won the Scottish title, the first time they had been able to clinch it at Celtic Park.

V IS FOR VERY FIRST MATCH
Celtic FC was founded in 1887 and their first ever game was against Rangers (of course!) in May 1888. The Bhoys ran out impressive 5-2 winners.

W IS FOR WIM JANSEN
The Dutch manager took Celtic to their first league title success in ten years in 1998. Sadly he then resigned after a bust up with the club's board of directors. His successor, Dr Josef Venglos, a Czech, was unable to repeat Jansen's success and was replaced as manager after one season.

X IS FOR Neuchatel XAMAX
The name of the team responsible for inflicting Celtic's biggest ever defeat in Europe. The Swiss side thumped The Bhoys 5-1 at home in the UEFA Cup in 1991.

Y IS FOR YOUNGEST
Roy Aitken is the youngest player to make his Celtic debut in a competitive match. He was a substitute in a League Cup game with Stenhousemuir in 1975. At the time he was still two months away from his 17th birthday. Aitken went on to captain both The Bhoys and Scotland, spending 15 seasons at Celtic Park.

Z IS FOR ZERO
The number of defeats Celtic suffered on their way to the title in the 1897/98 season. The Bhoys won 15 games, drew the remaining three, scoring 56 goals in the process, with just 13 against. Not bad going, eh?

N

W

FAMOUS WINS
ARSENAL

TEAMS
LIVERPOOL v ARSENAL

MATCH
DIVISION ONE 1988/89

VENUE
ANFIELD

DATE
MAY 26, 1989

STORY

The closest title race in league history saw Arsenal travel to Anfield on the last day of the season needing to beat top-of-the-table Liverpool by two clear goals to clinch the championship. George Graham's men, who hadn't won at Anfield for 15 years, went one up through striker Alan Smith after 52 minutes, but deep into injury time it looked like The Reds would hang on. Then Gunners star Michael Thomas burst through the Liverpool defence following a pass from Alan Smith and flicked the ball past 'keeper Bruce Grobbelaar to claim a famous victory, breaking 'Pool hearts in the process.

FINAL SCORE
LIVERPOOL 0 ARSENAL 2

Striker Alan Smith scored Arsenal's first and set up Michael Thomas's last gasp title clincher.

Michael Thomas slots the ball past Bruce Grobelaar to destroy Liverpool's title dreams.

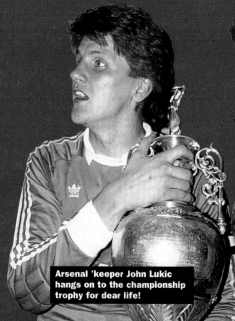

Arsenal 'keeper John Lukic hangs on to the championship trophy for dear life!

Arsenal celebrate their Division One championship victory at Anfield under George Graham.

Arsenal's Kevin Richardson gets stuck into Ronnie Whelan and Steve Staunton of Liverpool.

Tony Adams and John Aldridge tussle for the ball.

NIGEL MARTYN
LEEDS

For many Nigel was the outstanding 'keeper of last season and David Seaman is currently struggling to keep him out of England's No.1 shirt. Nige started his career with Bristol Rovers in 1987, before moving to Crystal Palace three years later. He spent seven seasons with The Eagles, making well over 200 first team appearances. He left for Elland Road in 1996 and hasn't looked back since.

THE STATS

- ☺ SUPPORTS BRISTOL ROVERS
- ☺ BORN ST AUSTELL 11/8/66
- ☺ HEIGHT 6ft 1in
- ☺ WEIGHT 14st 7lbs
- ☺ TEAMS BRISTOL ROVERS (1987-1990); CRYSTAL PALACE (1990-1996); LEEDS UNITED (1996-PRESENT)
- ☺ INTERNATIONAL STATUS FULL ENGLAND INTERNATIONAL – DEBUT v CIS, APRIL 29, 1992

1

IN AT THE DEEP END

In his first season at Palace, after joining the club from Bristol Rovers, Martin finds himself at Wembley in a FA Cup Final against Man United. An extraordinary first game ends 3-3 with Palace leading in extra-time. But United equalise and a Lee Martin goal settles the replay in their favour.

2

PALACE REACH THEIR ZENITH!

The season after Palace are back at Wembley and this time they're winners. The Zenith Data Systems trophy is hardly in the same class as the FA Cup but The Eagles don't care as they thump Everton 4-1, thanks to goals from John Salako, Geoff Thomas and Ian Wright (2).

5

BACK IN BUSINESS

Bigger clubs are rumoured to be set to sign Nigel but he sticks with Palace, helping them win promotion in 1994. They go back to the Premiership in style, as Champions.

13

6

ENGLAND CALLS

Nigel makes his debut for England while he's still a Palace player. He comes on as a sub in Moscow against the CIS in a friendly, but wins his full debut against Hungary on May 12, 1992.

7

MANCS RUFFLE EAGLES' FEATHERS

Manchester United prove to be Palace's stumbling block to glory again in 1995. The two teams lock horns in the FA Cup Semi-Finals and once again The Eagles go down after a replay. So near and yet so far...

Shoot

3

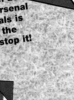

4

PAINFUL PENALTIES

Palace's fine run in the cups continues in 1992, but an old team-mate returns to haunt Nigel as The Eagles crash out of the League Cup to Arsenal in the Semi-Finals. One of The Gunners' goals is scored by ex-Palace man Ian Wright from the penalty spot, and Nige can do nothing to stop it!

RELEGATION BLUES

The Eagles suffer the agony of relegation at the end of the 1992/93 season. The south Londoners actually finish level on points with Oldham, who avoid the drop, but having only scored 48 goals in 42 games fall through the trapdoor into Division One.

8

THE EXIT

Palace go down again at the end of the 1994/95 season and are robbed of a top-flight place the following season in the Play-Off Final against Leicester. After seven loyal seasons with The Eagles, Martyn decides to move for the sake of his England career (he hasn't been capped since 1993). Leeds step in to sign him for £2.25 million.

10

RED CARD SHAME!

Leeds defeat Oxford 4-0 in the FA Cup Third Round in January 1998. But the win is spoiled by Nigel's sending-off in the last minute, after he'd sprinted out of his area to block U's sub Jamie Cooke, who was through on goal. Martyn had previously made two blinding saves from Nigel Jemson and Les Robinson.

HE'S A LEEDS MAN!

In his first season at Elland Road Martyn misses just one League game but his team can't finish higher than 11th. Despite that, Martyn has a good season between the sticks and receives an England recall against South Africa.

9

NIGEL MARTYN

LEEDS

ENGLAND DREAM

11

Now firmly established with United, Martyn sees off the challenges of Ian Walker and Tim Flowers to secure the England No.2 slot behind David Seaman. Prior to the World Cup Finals boss Glenn Hoddle gives Martyn a few chances to prove himself between the sticks and he keeps clean sheets against Cameroon and Belgium.

BIDING HIS TIME

12

Unsurprisingly Nigel goes to France '98. He doesn't take part in any of the matches but clearly finds the tournament a terrific experience. As Seaman comes towards the end of a glittering international career all eyes are on Big Nige to finally make the England No.1 shirt his, especially with Leeds flying high in the Premiership for the first time in years.

BACK IN EUROPE!

14

Leeds go from strength to strength in 1999, ending the season in fourth place, with another crack at the UEFA Cup their reward. They also ruin Arsenal's title ambitions by defeating The Gunners 1-0 at Elland Road.

ROLLED OVER BY ROMA

13

In the UEFA Cup Second Round Leeds come up against AS Roma of Italy. They lose the first-leg 1-0, but battle hard in the return at Elland Road. Sadly they can't find a way past the mean Roma defence and they go out 1-0 on aggregate.

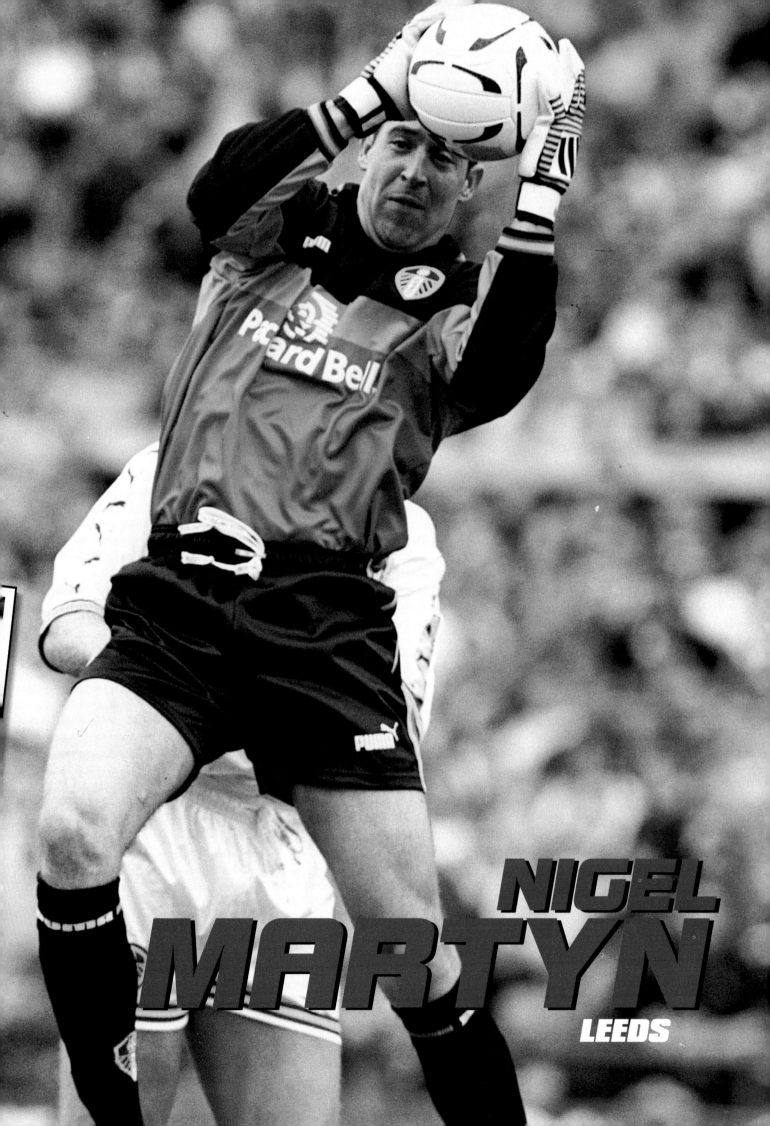

NIGEL MARTYN

LEEDS

a legend from the Wanderers' past, a hero from their present and a young star to watch in the future.

PRESENT

MICHAEL JOHANSEN

The diminutive winger won the hearts of supporters last term, bagging the club's Player Of The Season award after a series of exciting performances out on the right of midfield. Signed from Copenhagen in the summer of 1996 for £1 million, the great Dane took time to settle in at the Reebok, but rewarded boss Colin Todd's faith and contributed greatly to the Lancashire club's narrowly unsuccessful promotion bid.

PAST

ALAN STUBBS

Powerhouse defender from the era most fondly remembered by fans. Stubbs was the commanding lynchpin of the side which stormed its way up two divisions and brushed aside some of the best sides in the land in a series of heart-stopping cup runs. Liverpool-born Stubbs was inevitably courted by many top clubs before eventually heading north of the border with Celtic, where he inspired The Bhoys to their first League title for 10 years.

PAST PRESENT BOLTO

FUTURE

RICARDO GARDENER

A 19-year-old Jamaican World Cup star of great promise, who can play at full back or on the left side of midfield. Gardener is adjusting to life in the north west and will be looking to build on a promising debut season. Already has over 30 caps for Jamaica, and has been an established figure on the international scene since the age of 16.

FUTURE

A TO Z CFC

A IS FOR AWFUL
The way in which The Blues played on September 26, 1953 when they lost 8-1 to Wolves in Division One. It's Chelsea's worst ever defeat in any game.

B IS FOR BEARD
Like the one modelled by Chelsea chairman Ken Bates. Bates became chairman of Chelsea in 1982 when he bought the club for just a quid. Since then he's turned The Blues into one of Europe's biggest and best clubs.

C IS FOR COINCIDENCE
Chelsea met Middlesbrough in the 1997 FA Cup final and beat them 2-0. The teams met again the following year in the League Cup final – Chelsea won 2-0 again!

D IS FOR DRAKE'S DUCKLINGS
The nickname of the young Chelsea side which won the club's only league title in 1955. Ted Drake was the name of their manager.

E IS FOR EUROPE
Chelsea boss Gianluca Vialli is one of only a handful of stars who has won all three major European club competitions as a player – the European Cup, the UEFA Cup and the Cup Winners' Cup.

F IS FOR FA CUP
A trophy Chelsea have won twice. The first time in 1970 when they beat Leeds after a replay and again in 1997 when they defeated Middlesbrough.

G IS FOR GOING DOWN
Chelsea may be one of the Prem's high-fliers now but that hasn't always been the case. The Blues have been relegated from the country's top division on six occasions – in 1910, 1924, 1962, 1975, 1979 and 1988.

H IS FOR HOLLAND
the country ex-Blues boss Ruud Gullit is from. Ruudi joined Chelsea as a player in 1995 and became player/manager a year later. Thanks to Ruud, Chelsea won the FA Cup in 1997, their first major trophy in 26 years.

I IS FOR ITALIANS
Gianluca Vialli became the first ever Italian star to join The Blues when he signed in 1996. He was quickly joined by Zola, Di Matteo and Casiraghi.

J IS FOR JIMMY GREAVES
He notched 41 league goals for The Blues in the 1960-61 season. It's a tally that has never been bettered at Stamford Bridge.

K IS FOR 'KEEPER
Chelsea's very first goalie was William 'Fatty' Foulke. He was six feet two inches tall and weighed 22 stone! He also saved the very first penalty Chelsea ever conceded – at Stockport in September 1905.

L IS FOR Brian LAUDRUP
Certainly not the most popular player in Chelsea history. He quit the club last season just three months after joining The Blues on a free transfer from Rangers. He said he was homesick for Denmark!

M IS FOR MOST APPEARANCES
Infamous tough-tackling defender Ron 'Chopper' Harris has made more appearances for Chelsea than any other player – 795 between 1962 and 1980.

N IS FOR NICKNAMES
Chelsea's hasn't always been The Blues. For many years the club was also known as The Pensioners, in honour of the famous Chelsea Pensioners, old war

CHELSEA ★★★

A HISTORY OF THE BLUES – ALL THE WAY FROM A TO Z!

heroes who can still be seen at Stamford Bridge on matchdays in their bright red jackets.

O IS FOR OLYMPICS
Chelsea star Celestine Babayaro won an Olympic gold medal in 1996. He was part of the Nigerian footie team which beat Argentina to take the top spot. He even scored in the final!

P IS FOR PETER OSGOOD
According to many he is Chelsea's greatest ever player. Ozzy was a Blues hero in the late '60s and early '70s, scoring 150 goals in 380 league games. He's also scored more goals in European matches than any other Chelsea star – 16. Despite his success as a club player, Ozzy only ever played four times for England.

Q IS FOR QUICKEST GOAL
Roberto Di Matteo's strike at Wembley in 1997 is the quickest FA Cup final goal of the 20th century, timed at just 42 seconds. Di Matteo was signed for The Blues by Ruud Gullit from Lazio in 1996.

R IS FOR REAL MADRID
The team Chelsea beat to lift the European Cup Winners' Cup trophy for the first time in 1971.

The Blues beat the Spanish giants again in 1998 to claim the European Super Cup.

S IS FOR STAMFORD BRIDGE
Chelsea's home since 1905. The site was originally developed in 1876 as an athletics ground, and wasn't used for football until 1905. The ground's owner, Mr H. A. Mears, had offered it to Fulham originally, but they turned it down. Determined to use the site for football, he decided to form his own team – and Chelsea were born!

T IS FOR THREE
The number of league games lost by Chelsea last season. But such an impressive record wasn't enough to see The Blues finish any higher than third behind Man United and Arsenal.

U IS FOR UNBELIEVABLE
In 1997 Chelsea were 2-0 down against Liverpool at half-time in the fourth round of the FA Cup at Stamford Bridge. They bounced back to win 4-2 thanks to goals by Hughes, Zola and Vialli (2).

V IS FOR Terry VENABLES
Believe it or not the former England and Spurs boss started his playing career at Stamford

Bridge. He was part of The Blues' side which won the League Cup in 1965 over two legs against Leeds.

W IS FOR Ray WILKINS
Chelsea's most capped player. 'Butch' made 24 England appearances while resident at The Bridge. As a player he went onto star for Man United and AC Milan and to manage QPR and Fulham.

X IS FOR XMAS
Back in the 1950s league matches used to be played on Christmas day. On December 25, 1957 The Blues took on Portsmouth at Stamford Bridge and shared an amazing 11 goals with them. Chelsea were the winners – 7-4!

Y IS FOR YOBS
In the 1980s Chelsea had a big problem with football hooligans. So much so in fact that chairman Ken Bates erected an electrified fence between the terraces and the pitch to keep 'em in check!

Z IS FOR Gianfranco ZOLA
The little Italian who joined The Blues in 1996 from Parma. He was named the Footballer Of The Year in 1997 and scored Chelsea's winner in the Cup Winners' Cup final against Stuttgart the following year – 17 seconds after coming on as a sub!

J

O

W

FAMOUS WINS
NEWCASTLE

TEAMS
NEWCASTLE v MAN UNITED

MATCH
PREMIERSHIP FIXTURE

VENUE
ST JAMES' PARK

DATE
OCTOBER 20, 1996

STORY

Kevin Keegan's team had a couple of reasons to hate Man United. Firstly, The Reds had steamed in to steal the Premiership title from under Geordie noses the previous season and had thumped them 4-0 in the Charity Shield. Suffice to say a few scores were settled at St James' Park as Newcastle inflicted United's biggest league loss in 12 years – and their first defeat in the Prem all season. Toon were two up at half-time through Darren Peacock and David Ginola, while Les Ferdinand, Alan Shearer and Philippe Albert struck in the second half to complete the rout. The result was enough to put Toon top of the table although their stay at the summit was brief.

FINAL SCORE
NEWCASTLE 5 UNITED 0

Ferdinand, Batty and Shearer in celebratory mood.

Toon take the lead thanks to Darren Peacock.

Newcastle's 5-0 win wasn't enough to prevent United retaining their Premiership title.

Eric Cantona's miserable afternoon is complete as he picks up a yellow card.

David Ginola, the scorer of Toon's second goal, holds off a challenge from Gary Neville.

ANDREI KANCHELSKIS
RANGERS

The Russian superstar has been showing the other wingers in Europe how to play down the line for years. He was tearing defences to pieces five years ago at Manchester United and was an inspiration to the likes of the young Ryan Giggs. He quit Everton for Serie A side Fiorentina in 1997 but returned to Britain a year later to help Rangers win a Scottish treble.

HATS OFF TO ANDREI

The lightning quick winger spends his early days with Russian sides Dynamo Kiev and Donetsk. It isn't long, however, before his special talent is noticed by the big clubs across Europe, including Manchester United, who snap him up for £650,000 in March 1991 after he impresses Alex Ferguson during a one week trial.

PLAYING FOR THE MOTHERLAND

Although born in the Ukraine Andrei chooses to play for Russia after the break up of the Soviet Union. He plays his first international game for his country in August 1989, coming on as a substitute against Poland at the age of 20. He becomes a regular in the national team for the next decade.

PENALTY!

The following season United claim their first league and cup double. They take the title by eight clear points and a Kanchelskis goal against Oldham puts them in the FA Cup Final with Chelsea. Andrei makes an impact in the Final too, winning a penalty which French star Eric Cantona duly converts.

MISSING THE WORLD CUP IN '94

On the way to the World Cup in 1994, Russia meet France and Andrei hooks up with his United team-mate Eric Cantona. Russia go on to qualify for the tournament in the States but Kanchelskis rules himself out of selection for the squad after having a series of arguments with the team's management.

THE STATS

- SUPPORTS DYNAMO KIEV
- BORN KIROWGRAD, UKRAINE
- HEIGHT 5ft 8ins
- WEIGHT 12st 4lbs
- TEAMS DYNAMO KIEV ['87-89]; DONEZTS (1989-91); MAN UNITED (1991-95); EVERTON (1996-97); FIORENTINA (1997-98); RANGERS (98-PRESENT)
- INTERNATIONAL STATUS FULL RUSSIA INTERNATIONAL – DEBUT v POLAND, AUGUST 1989

DOUBLE WINNER

Despite being 0-0 at half-time United go on to win the Final 4-0, clinching their double success and denying Chelsea their first piece of major silverware since 1971. Kanchelskis is on top of the world.

Shoot

A UNITED REGULAR

He becomes a regular fixture in the Man United side during his first full season at Old Trafford (1991/92), notching 34 league appearances and five goals. But Fergie's boys narrowly miss out on the title after being pipped by Leeds in the last few games of the season.

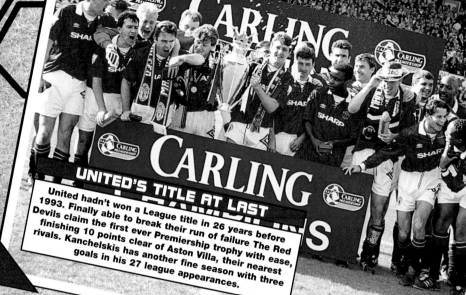

UNITED'S TITLE AT LAST

United hadn't won a League title in 26 years before 1993. Finally able to break their run of failure The Red Devils claim the first ever Premiership trophy with ease, finishing 10 points clear of Aston Villa, their nearest rivals. Kanchelskis has another fine season with three goals in his 27 league appearances.

UNITED EXIT

Andrei's time at United ends under a cloud as Fergie opts to sell him to Everton after a series of bust ups between the two men. He moves to Goodison for £5 million in the summer of 1995 after protracted transfer negotiations which, at one point, even involve his former club Donetsk, who stand to make money on the move thanks to a special sell-on clause in his United contract.

BOMBIN' OUT AT EURO '96

After sitting out World Cup '94 Kanchelskis is a key part of the Russian squad for Euro '96 held in England. But the Russians are placed in a tough group with Italy, Czech Republic and the eventual winners Germany. Despite being touted as a major force in the competition they bomb out, coming last in their group.

MERSEYSIDE

Andrei enjoys his first season with The Toffees. He finishes as Everton's top scorer with 17 goals, despite missing the club's first few games of the season due to the transfer wrangle with United. His first goals come in the 2-0 derby win over Liverpool.

ANDREI KANCHELSKIS

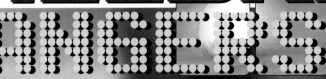

OFF TO ITALY

Kanchelskis quits Goodison Park to join Italian giants Fiorentina for £8 million in January 1997. The Italian fans can't wait to watch him destroy full backs as he did in England but he has trouble settling and suffers with injuries. Strangley he says he misses Britain and even the Manchester rain!

11

12

ANDREI'S A TRUE BRIT!

After barely a year in Italy Andrei returns to Britain as part of Dick Advocaat's rebuilding job at Rangers. His transfer fee, £5.5 million, is a Scottish record at the time. After a slow start he begins to settle in and helps the Scottish giants progress in the UEFA Cup with a goal against Salonika in a 2-0 win.

13

BACK ON THE TROPHY TRAIL

Rangers had finished the previous season potless, so it wasn't just Andrei who was delighted when his team defeated St Johnstone 2-1 to claim victory in the Scottish League Cup Final. It was their first trophy in what was to become a landmark season for the club.

14

THE TITLE AT CELTIC PARK

Rangers finished the season in fine style. They beat Celtic 3-0 to claim the Scottish title on their rivals' home ground for the first time. To add insult to injury they also beat The Bhoys 1-0 in the Scottish Cup Final to clinch a treble.

ANDREI KANCHELSKI

RANGERS

PAST

KENNY DALGLISH

Arguably the greatest star in Liverpool's history, Kenny joined the Merseyside club from Celtic at the age of 27 in 1977 for £400,000, having already achieved untold glory in Glasgow. What followed was a fairy-tale run of success where the Scot won six League titles, three European Cups, four League Cups and an FA cup for good measure. On the way he also scored 168 goals, before winning a league and cup double as 'Pool manager in 1986.

shoot presents a legend from Anfield's past, a hero from its present and a talented youngster to watch for the future!

PAST PRESENT
LIVER

FUTURE

JAMIE CARRAGHER

One of the few bright spots of last season for The Reds was the emergence of 20-year-old central defender Carragher. Another graduate of Liverpool's successful youth academy the battling youngster has added some much needed steel to 'Pool's backline. England recognition at Under-21 level has followed his regular appearances in the Anfield first team.

PRESENT

MICHAEL OWEN

Liverpool may not have had the easiest of rides over the last few seasons but their discovery of young Michael has to be the find of the century. The 20-year-old Chester born striker is best known for his World Cup Finals goal against Argentina in 1998 but his regular scoring heroics for Liverpool shouldn't be forgotten either. He's banged in 46 goals for The Reds in all competitions in the last two seasons making him the Prem's most consistent hitman.

FUTURE
POOL

A TO Z

SOUTHAMPTON FC

A IS FOR ALAN BALL
The 1966 World Cup winner joined Saints in 1977 and his 'never say die' attitude helped the club back into the top flight a year later. He returned as manager in 1994.

B IS FOR BROTHERS
On October 22, 1988, Southampton became the first side to field three brothers in a match for 68 years. They were Ray, Rod and Danny Wallace and they lined up against Sheff Wed at the Dell. The Saints won 2-1.

C IS FOR CUP HERO
Bobby Stokes' legendary goal at Wembley against Man United on May 1, 1976, took the FA Cup to The Dell for the first and only time. The tiny striker scored 52 goals during eight years at the club.

D IS FOR the DROP
Despite a seemingly annual battle against relegation, Southampton have only been relegated twice in their history.

E IS FOR EARLY DAYS
Southampton FC was formed in 1885 as Southampton St Marys, which explains the origins of their nickname, The Saints. But it wasn't until 1920 that the club joined the football league.

F IS FOR FLOODLIGHTS
Southampton were the first team to play under floodlights in England, when they were erected at The Dell in 1951.

G IS FOR GUERNSEY
The birthplace of Saints idol, Matt Le Tissier, perhaps the most naturally gifted player to don the famous red and white striped shirt. He made his debut for Saints in 1986 and has been there ever since!

H IS FOR HORSE-RACING
Mick Channon, who has scored more goals for Saints than anyone else (215), will always be remembered at The Dell for his windmill-arm goal celebrations. He's now a successful racehorse trainer.

I IS FOR INTERNATIONAL CAPS
Peter Shilton won more caps as a Southampton player than any other in the club's history. The top 'keeper played for Southampton between 1982 and 1987 and played for England 49 times while a Southampton player.

J IS FOR Dave JONES
The current Saints boss. A promising youngster with Everton and Coventry, Jones' career was cut short by injury. He won promotion as manager of Stockport County in 1997, joining Southampton shortly afterwards.

K IS FOR KNIGHTHOOD
England's World Cup winning manager, Sir Alf Ramsey, joined Southampton as a player whilst in the army in 1946. Unable to establish himself in the first team he quit for Tottenham in May, 1949.

L IS FOR LONG-SERVING BOSS
Lawrie McMenemy is one of Saints' longest-serving and most successful managers. He took over in 1974, leading the club to FA Cup glory in 1976 and promotion to the top-flight two years later. Under McMenemy the club finished as title runners-up to Liverpool in 1984.

M IS FOR MARKSMAN
England captain Alan Shearer started his career at Southampton, and made his first start against Arsenal in 1988.

B

G

H

SOUTHAMPTON

He caused an absolute sensation that day, by becoming the youngest ever player to score a hat-trick in a league game. Super Al left The Dell in 1992 for Blackburn Rovers.

N IS FOR NICKNAMES
During the 1970s, Southampton acquired a new nickname. After a particularly bruising encounter with Liverpool, Reds boss Bill Shankly described the side from The Dell as the Ale House Brawlers, a name which stuck for some years.

O IS FOR OH DEAR!
Saints' worst defeat is 8-0, a scoreline suffered against both Spurs and Everton.

P IS FOR Terry PAINE
The versatile winger's 713 appearances for The Saints between 1956 and 1974 is a club record.

Q IS FOR QUIZ QUESTION
When was the one and only international played at The Dell? It was way back in 1901 when England played Ireland.

R IS FOR RESULT!
The best scoreline the Saints have managed in recent years must be their 6-3 mauling of Champions Man United on October 26, 1996. Helped by Roy Keane's sending off in the first half, Egil Ostenstad helped himself to a hat-trick, Israeli Eyal Berkovic scored twice, with Matt le Tissier netting the other goal.

S IS FOR transfer SCOOP
When Lawrie McMenemy signed Kevin Keegan for 400,000 in July 1980, he probably got himself the bargain of the decade. The twice-European Footballer Of The Year finished as the top-flight's top scorer in 1981-82 with 28 goals and won the PFA Player Of The Year award.

T IS FOR TRANSFER RECORD
When striker Kevin Davies left Saints for Blackburn in the summer of 1998, the club received £7 million for the sale, a club record.

U IS FOR UNFINISHED BUSINESS
The harsh winter of 1963 took its toll on football fixtures. Southampton's Third Round tie at home to York City was postponed nine times before finally going ahead on February 13! Saints eventually won 5-0.

V IS FOR VENUE OF LEGENDS
Also known as Wembley Stadium. The Saints' last appearance there came when they stepped out to play Nott'm Forest in the 1979 League Cup Final. It was not a happy day, Forest won 3-1.

W IS FOR Steve WILLIAMS
Regarded as one of the best players who ever graced the Southampton midfield, Steve Williams played 335 games between 1976 and 1984 including the 1979 League Cup Final before moving on to Arsenal in December 1984.

X IS FOR EX-DEFENDER
Mark Wright enjoyed five years at Southampton between 1982 and 1987, establishing himself as an England regular. He went on to play for Liverpool and in 1990 helped England to the World Cup semi-finals.

Y IS FOR YOUNGEST PLAYER
The youngest player to appear for The Saints is Danny Wallace, who made his debut against Man United on November 29, 1980, aged 16 years and 313 days.

Z IS FOR ZERO
The number of wins Saints had enjoyed after their first nine Premiership games last season. They finally broke the spell by beating Coventry 2-1.

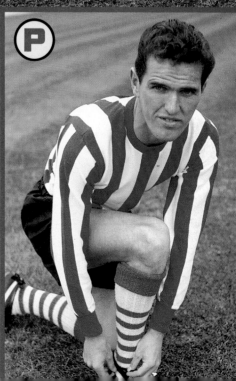

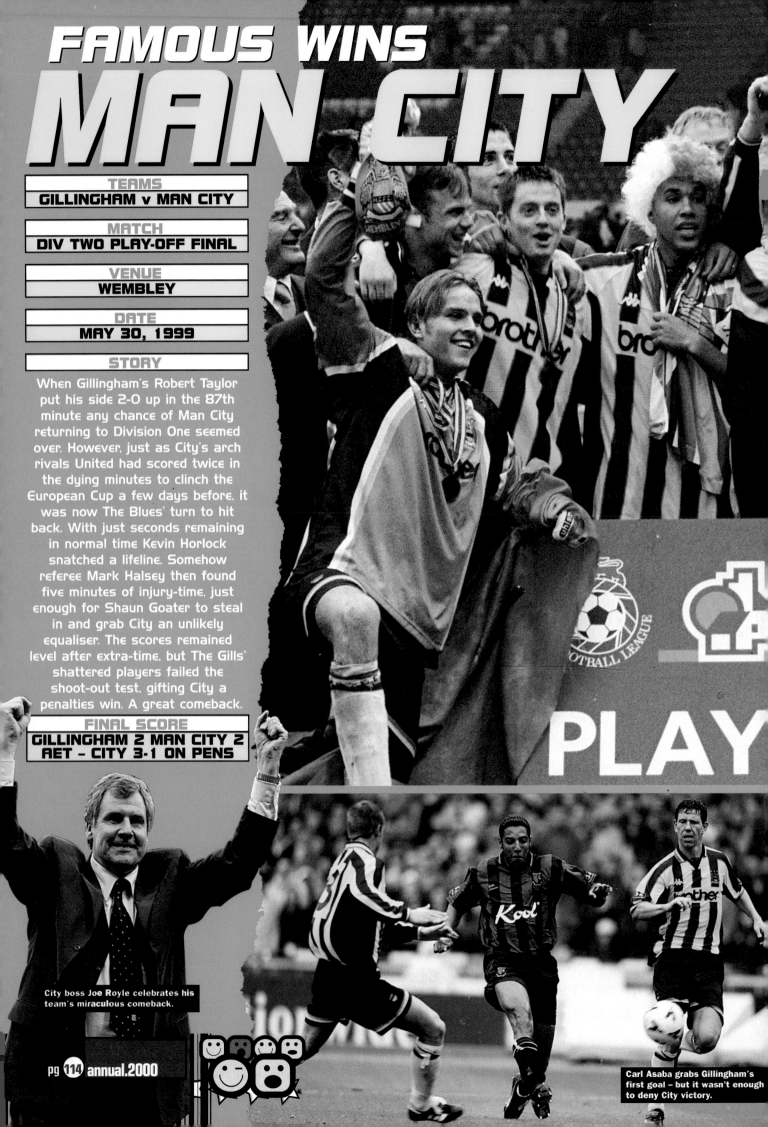

FAMOUS WINS
MAN CITY

TEAMS
GILLINGHAM v MAN CITY

MATCH
DIV TWO PLAY-OFF FINAL

VENUE
WEMBLEY

DATE
MAY 30, 1999

STORY
When Gillingham's Robert Taylor put his side 2-0 up in the 87th minute any chance of Man City returning to Division One seemed over. However, just as City's arch rivals United had scored twice in the dying minutes to clinch the European Cup a few days before, it was now The Blues' turn to hit back. With just seconds remaining in normal time Kevin Horlock snatched a lifeline. Somehow referee Mark Halsey then found five minutes of injury-time, just enough for Shaun Goater to steal in and grab City an unlikely equaliser. The scores remained level after extra-time, but The Gills' shattered players failed the shoot-out test, gifting City a penalties win. A great comeback.

FINAL SCORE
GILLINGHAM 2 MAN CITY 2
AET – CITY 3-1 ON PENS

City boss **Joe Royle** celebrates his team's miraculous comeback.

PLAY

Carl Asaba grabs Gillingham's first goal – but it wasn't enough to deny City victory.

Man City celebrate their return to Division One following an unlikely victory over Gillingham at Wembley.

Nationwide

OFF WINNERS

The City boys go crazy after their penalties win over the unlucky Gills.

Penalties hero and City 'keeper Nicky Weaver with the play-off trophy.

ALAN SHEARER
NEWCASTLE

Although critics don't think Alan Shearer is the player he once was, there's no doubt that he's one of the best strikers ever produced in England. Having started his career with Southampton, Shearer was snapped up by big-spending Blackburn Rovers in 1992. He went on to score 112 goals in 138 appearances and led them to the league title in 1995. He joined Newcastle for £15 million in 1996.

THE STATS

⚽ **SUPPORTS** NEWCASTLE
⚽ **BORN** NEWCASTLE 13/8/70
⚽ **HEIGHT** 5ft 10ins
⚽ **WEIGHT** 12st 6lbs
⚽ **TEAMS** SOUTHAMPTON (1987-92); BLACKBURN (1992-96); NEWCASTLE (1996-PRESENT)
⚽ **INTERNATIONAL STATUS** CAPTAIN OF ENGLAND – DEBUT v FRANCE, FEBRUARY 1992

1

LIFE WITH THE SAINTS

Somehow Alan escaped the clutches of the top flight's biggest teams and began his career with Southampton in 1987. Not one to waste time, Shearer made his debut against Arsenal and blew them away with a hat-trick. He oozed quality and the team on the south-coast knew their troubles were no longer about staying in the top flight but keeping their young star.

2

ENGLAND CALLS

The phone soon rings to invite Shearer to join up with the international squad. If there were any fears that he wouldn't be able to cut it at the very highest level they are soon blasted away as the Geordie gets on the score sheet with one of his idols Gary Lineker in a 2-0 victory over France.

6

A FAMILY MAN

When he isn't banging in the goals for Blackburn Shearer likes nothing more than spending time with his young family. Here's his wife, Lainya, who he met when he was a YTS trainee at Southampton. and two kids, Chloe and Hollie, helping Alan enjoy Blackburn's title success in 1995.

7

BACK HOME

Despite massive interest from Man United Shearer decides to quit Blackburn for the team he supported as a boy – Newcastle. He joins the Geordies in a deal worth £15 million and thousands of Magpies fans turn up at St James' Park to welcome him.

5 ## THE GERMANS

The semi-final against Germany has the lot except an England victory. Shearer puts Venables' men ahead early on from a header following a corner. But the Germans level it through Kuntz and eventually win 6-5 on penalties. Shearer is the tournament's top scorer with five goals but it's little consolation.

Shoot

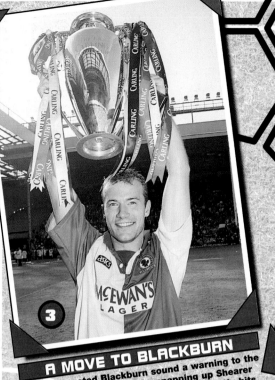

3

A MOVE TO BLACKBURN

Newly-promoted Blackburn sound a warning to the rest of the Premiership by snapping up Shearer from The Saints for £3.3 million in 1992. He hits 30 goals three seasons running and helps Rovers to glory in 1995 when they take the league title for the first time since 1914.

4

ENGLAND EURO '96

Shearer becomes the first name on manager Terry Venables' England team list going into the European Championships in 1996. He scores in the draw against Switzerland and the win against Scotland. He then bags another two as England totally dismantle a poor Holland side 4-1. Venables' team roar into the semi-finals for a date with destiny against old enemy Germany at Wembley Stadium.

8

THE GOLDEN BOOT

Different team but it's the same result for hot-shot Shearer. He hits 25 goals in 31 league appearances for Newcastle during the 1996/97 season, giving him his fourth Golden Boot award in a row. Sadly, Newcastle once again finish runners-up in the league, as Man United take top spot. However, it does mean that they qualify for the Champions League for the first time!

9

WORLD CUP QUEST

With the disappointment of Euro '96 still hurting Shearer, the now England captain is determined to make sure his side don't fail in their quest to make it to the World Cup in France. Super Al scores five times in the qualifiers, including a crucial double at Wembley against Poland.

LIVING WITH THE LEGENDS

Shearer's form for club and country is properly recognised in 1997, as the Newcastle & England hero is named the world's third best player. AC Milan's George Weah and Ronaldo, then of Barcelona, top the poll. One or two fans on Tyneside might have disagreed with that order though!

10

ALAN SHEARER

NEWCASTLE UNITED

MORE AWARDS

There's little surprise when the Geordie genius picks up a couple more trophies in 1997 – the PFA Player Of The Year award and the Sports Writers' Player Of The Year award. In five seasons he's scored a breathtaking 137 goals in 169 league appearances!

11

12

SUPER AL OUT OF ACTION

Things went pear-shaped for Super Al just a couple of weeks before the 1997/98 season began. Playing in a friendly against Chelsea for Newcastle the super striker badly damaged his ankle when he slipped trying to get a loose ball. The injury meant that he missed almost five months of the new season.

13

14

MORE PENALTIES DESPAIR

It was time for some more England heartache at the World Cup Finals in France. Glenn Hoddle's men rarely looked like world beaters and were defeated early on by Romania. They were ultimately dumped out of the competition by Argentina at the second round stage, once again on penalties!

DOUBLE FA CUP HEARTBREAK

Wembley may have been a happy hunting ground for Shearer whenever he has pulled on an England shirt but the same certainly can't be said for his experiences of the grand old stadium with Newcastle. The Magpies have lost two FA Cup Finals in a row in the last two seasons, firstly to Arsenal then to Man United. Shearer and Newcastle haven't been able to score in either game, which have both finished 2-0.

ALAN SHEARER

NEWCASTLE

THE CRUNCH

OK, Shoot readers, better prepare yourselves for the ultimate test of your footie knowledge. Over the next eight pages the Crunch will test you to the max with tough quiz questions, perplexing puzzles and tricky conundrums galore! We want to find out just how much you know about football in this country, in Europe and the world! Once you've waded through each tough-tackling section you can check your answers, add up your scores and see how you rate on the Crunch Counter (page 127). It will tell you whether you're a top footie brainbox or whether you should try a different sport - like five-a-side knitting - instead! Have fun and get Crunching!

TROPHY TRAIL

SEEING AS HOW THIS IS THE FIRST ROUND, WE'VE DECIDED TO MAKE IT EASY. JUST SEE IF YOU CAN NAME EACH PICTURED TROPHY FROM THE CLUES PROVIDED. PIECE OF CAKE, WE RECKON!

ONE POINT FOR EACH CORRECT ANSWER

2 THIS TROPHY WAS FIRST CONTESTED IN 1872 WHEN IT WAS WON BY A TEAM CALLED WANDERERS.

1 THE FIRST TEAM TO WIN THIS TROPHY AND THE LAST TEAM TO WIN IT ARE ONE AND THE SAME.

3 THE CURRENT HOLDERS OF THIS TROPHY SCORED TWO INJURY-TIME GOALS TO WIN IT BACK IN MAY.

4 THIS TROPHY NO LONGER EXISTS, BUT THE LAST BRITISH SIDE TO WIN IT ARE A LONDON CLUB WHO PLAY IN BLUE.

THE MISSING LINK

CAN YOU REPLACE THE MISSING NAMES THAT COMPLETE THESE TALES FROM LAST SEASON?

1. Because he scored the most goals in the least amount of games, _Owen_ won last season's Golden Boot

2. After a long zig-zagging run, _Giggs_ blasted the ball past Seaman in last season's FA Cup Semi-Final

3. The Sunderland striker, _Phillips_ joined the England squad for their match against Hungary.

4. Ex-Nott'm Forest hero, _Campbell_, joined Everton from Trabzonspor on loan.

5. The Hammers' top scorer, _Wright_, smashed up the ref's changing room after being sent off.

6. _Petit_, Arsenal's tough-tackling French midfielder saw red at Goodison Park.

ONE POINT FOR EACH CORRECT ANSWER

PLAYER WORD SEARCH

P	C	O	D	E	S	C	H	A	M	P	S
O	O	J	V	I	E	Y	I	J	H	K	L
P	L	Y	P	O	Y	M	B	D	V	M	H
I	E	T	E	S	C	M	A	H	I	S	E
L	M	H	A	T	O	O	R	S	E	D	S
A	A	P	C	Y	O	N	T	I	I	F	K
M	N	G	R	A	Y	S	O	N	R	B	E
P	A	O	O	L	R	R	N	L	A	C	Y
A	H	H	O	Y	E	R	O	P	K	O	G
R	D	I	C	H	I	O	B	E	R	H	H
D	F	G	W	H	K	U	F	K	T	J	H
E	P	H	F	O	W	L	E	R	B	A	R

Poyet, Coleman, Lampard, Grayson, Deschamps, Barton, Heskey, Vieira, Yorke, Carr, Dichio, Fowler

ONE POINT FOR EACH HIDDEN NAME FOUND

THE MOVERS & SHAKERS

MOST PLAYERS MOVE FROM CLUB TO CLUB EVERY NOW AND THEN. CAN YOU IDENTIFY THESE STARS JUST BY LOOKING AT WHERE THEY'VE PLAYED?

1. Luton Town > Arsenal > West Ham > Wimbledon _____

2. Middlesbrough > Man United > Middlesbrough _____

3. Watford > Liverpool > Newcastle > Charlton > Celtic _____

4. Leeds United > Blackburn > Newcastle > Leeds United _____

5. West Brom > Liverpool > West Ham > Everton > Coventry _____

6. Arsenal > Nottingham Forest > Trabzonspor > Everton _____

7. Doncaster Rovers > Sheff United > Leeds United > Sheff United > Benfica > Middlesbrough _____

8. Toulon > Racing Paris > Brest > Paris St Germain > Newcastle > Tottenham _____

9. Man United > Barcelona > Man United > Chelsea > Southampton _____

10. West Ham > Man United > Inter Milan > Liverpool _____

ONE POINT FOR EACH CORRECT ANSWER

STRIP OFF

CAN YOU NAME THESE SIX PLAYERS WHO WE'VE PICTURED OUT OF THEIR FOOTIE KITS?

ONE POINT FOR EACH CORRECT ANSWER

STRIP OFF

CAN YOU NAME THESE SIX PLAYERS WHO WE'VE PICTURED OUT OF THEIR FOOTIE KITS?

ONE POINT FOR EACH CORRECT ANSWER

David B

_D___

Cole

Fowler

Morrien

CRYPTIC NAMES

SEE IF YOU CAN GUESS EACH PLAYER'S SURNAME BY WORKING OUT THE CRYPTIC CLUES. E.G. UNDERMOON = OVERMARS, GEDDIT? WE'VE EVEN GIVEN YOU EACH STARS TEAM TO HELP YOU FURTHER!

Undermoon (Arsenal) _____
Westdoor (Aston Villa) _____
Landwoman (Arsenal) _____
Liquidnote (Middlesbrough) _____
Labradorless (Aston Villa) _____
Candlesoft (West Ham) _____
Beanhen (Blackburn) _____
Whichdaughter (Aston Villa) _____
Whiteill (Middlesbrough) _____
Liverdaughter (Wimbledon) _____

FIVE POINTS FOR EACH ONE CORRECTLY ANSWERED

NAME THE NICKNAME

THIS ONE'S SIMPLE. WE'VE GIVEN YOU THE NAMES OF TEN CLUBS – ALL YOU HAVE TO DO IS GIVE US THEIR NICKNAMES.

Celtic _The Bhoys_
Fulham _The Cottages_
Sunderland _The Mackem_
Queens Park Rangers _The R_
Rochdale _The Dale_
Swansea City _The Swans_
Oxford United _The U's_
Plymouth Argyle _The Pilgrims_
Crystal Palace _The Eagles_
Derby County _The Ram_

ONE POINT FOR EACH CORRECT ANSWER

TEAM-MATE TWISTER

THE CRUNCH HAS MIXED UP TWO PLAYER'S NAMES. CAN YOU UNRAVEL THE LETTERS TO SEPARATE THEM INTO TWO TEAM-MATES?

aiLdVuasosnrk (Celtic) _____
npBgSaemnkaera (Arsenal) _____
rOrhagaeCwnre (Liverpool) _____
rhcostnteHTaahr (Wimbledon) _____
eennDudriilHb (Aston Villa) _____
tSleElagotva (Leicester) _____
yllMerBah (Everton) _____
ceWArebzallalt (Rangers) _____
yerrGoFeeDer (Chelsea) _____
nhtBoerAohtot (Sheff Wed) _____

ONE POINT FOR EACH CORRECT ANSWER

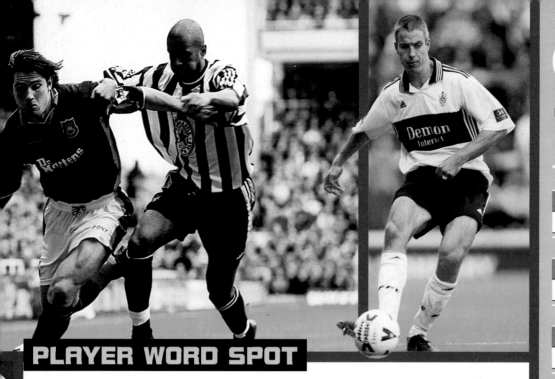

PLAYER WORD SPOT

T	S	S	D	B	M	S	H	O	N	S	T
C	C	C	K	O	E	F	V	I	D	D	T
Z	O	L	A	W	N	H	X	J	J	U	G
B	L	E	D	Y	D	U	K	N	O	B	R
F	E	T	C	E	O	O	E	E	O	L	F
H	S	R	N	R	N	R	D	F	A	I	D
J	O	U	G	E	C	A	R	B	O	N	E
D	U	A	G	K	A	D	T	S	T	D	E
A	L	D	Y	G	A	S	U	T	T	O	N
O	T	D	E	C	A	M	P	B	E	L	L
R	E	D	K	N	A	P	P	D	N	E	M
S	C	H	W	A	R	Z	E	R	E	F	M

Bergkamp, Flo, Zola, Carbone, Mendonca, Schwarzer, Dublin, Keane, Campbell, Redknapp, Bowyer, Sutton

ONE POINT FOR EACH HIDDEN NAME FOUND

DISTANT COUSINS?

THESE TOP FOOTIE PLAYERS SHARE THE SAME SURNAME – BUT THEY'RE NOT ALL RELATED. BY WORKING OUT THE CLUES SIMPLY GIVE US EACH PLAYER'S FIRST NAME.

1. CAMPBELL
- Defender for George Graham's Worthington Cup winners
- Striker for The Toffees
- _____

2. PEACOCK
- Defender for Ruud Gullit's Geordie side
- QPR's ex-Chelsea midfielder
- _____

3. FERDINAND
- West Ham's skillful centre-back
- The ex-England striker who's a bit good with his head
- _____

4. FERGUSON
- Gum-chewing manager of the Manchester Reds
- Imposing striker for The Toon
- _____

5. DYER
- Barnsley's ex-Crystal Palace striker
- The promising midfielder from Ipswich
- _____

6. ARMSTRONG
- Striker who once moved from Crystal Palace to Spurs
- Nottingham Forest midfielder
- _____

ONE POINT FOR EACH PAIR OF NAMES CORRECTLY IDENTIFIED

KING KEV'S QUIZ

KEVIN KEEGAN HAS PROVED HE'S THE MAN FOR ENGLAND'S TOP JOB. BUT WHEN IT COMES TO THE CRUNCH, WHAT DO YOU KNOW ABOUT THE GAME'S TOP GAFFER?

1. What year did King Kev quit playing football?_____

2. Which clubs did King Kev play for before he went into management?_____

3. Who were King Kev's first opponents as England boss and what was the score?_____

4. King Kev quote, but who was he talking about?: "If they cloned footballers he'd be the first you'd want in the lab."

_____

5. King Kev predicted that England were the only winners in one World Cup game at France '98, but who did England immediately go on to lose 2-1 to seconds afterwards?_____

6. Which side did King Kev take to Anfield twice and lose 4-3 on both occasions?_____

7. King Kev quote, but which manager was he fuming about?: "And I tell you what, after what he's done, I would love it if we beat them tonight, love it."_____

8. With which side did King Kev win the European Cup in 1977?_____

9. When was King Kev voted European Footballer Of The Year?_____

10. Which German club did King Kev join for £500,000 in 1977?_____

ONE POINT FOR EACH CORRECT ANSWER

GROUND TO A HALT

If you think you're doing well so far, then this should slow you down a bit. Can you name these top footie grounds just from their pictures?

ONE POINT FOR EACH GROUND CORRECTLY NAMED

CRYPTIC FOOTBALL CLUB

MORE CRYPTIC CRUNCH CONUNDRUMS FOR YOU TO GET STUCK INTO! WORK OUT EACH TRICKY CLUE TO GIVE YOU THE NAME OF A TOP BRITISH CLUB E.G. NUTOFF = BOLTON (BOLT-ON, GEDDIT?).

Nutoff _____

Woman Town _____

East Bacon _____

Emptybacon _____

Heartpuddle _____

Duckland Town _____

Babyninebacon _____

WhichBMW _____

Whitescold _____

Whitepuddle _____

ONE POINT FOR EACH CORRECT ANSWER

CLUB WORD SPOT

```
W  T  U  R  R  R  B  U  R  N  L  E  Y
A  R  S  E  N  A  L  K  I  P  V  O
L  S  D  V  B  N  G  V  E  R  E  W
S  C  H  E  L  S  E  A  F  L  R  W
A  W  U  Q  R  R  T  H  F  E  T  A
L  D  L  W  P  T  C  H  N  E  O  S
L  A  L  O  F  V  B  D  R  D  N  T
E  D  O  E  F  G  H  E  S  S  O
S  L  K  I  L  M  A  R  N  O  C  K
Q  S  C  V  B  N  G  B  W  R  G  E
C  O  V  E  N  T  R  Y  H  J  H  M
W  D  F  T  B  F  N  F  B  J  G  V
```

Leeds, Kilmarnock, Stoke, Derby, Coventry, Liverpool, Burnley, Chelsea, Everton, Hull, Walsall, Arsenal

ONE POINT FOR EACH HIDDEN NAME FOUND

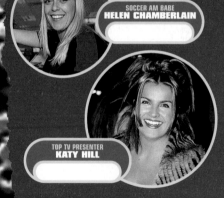

4

5

6

7

HIDDEN FACES

HEY, THIS ONE'S TOUGH. CAN YOU IDENTIFY EACH PLAYER EVEN THOUGH YOU CAN'T SEE THEIR FACES PROPERLY?

ONE POINT FOR EACH PLAYER YOU CORRECTLY IDENTIFY

1

Vialli

2

Leboeuf

3

Beckham

4

Dublin

5

Wright

6

R Ferdinand

7

Ginola

8

Blake

FOREIGN LEGION

WE ALL KNOW ABOUT THE FOREIGN PLAYERS AT TOP CLUBS IN BRITAIN BUT WHAT ABOUT THOSE BRITISH STARS WHO'VE PLAYED IN EUROPE? CAN YOU NAME THE COUNTRY THAT EACH STAR BELOW HAS PLAYED IN?

ONE POINT FOR EACH CORRECT ANSWER

1

2

3

4

5

6